BULLETPROOF SETUPS

29 Proven Stock Market Training Strategies

Matt Giannino

ISBN 978-1-7345540-0-7 (paperback)
ISBN 978-1-7345540-2-1 (e-book)

Giannino Products and Services
394 Cypress St.
Broomfield, CO 80020
www.marketmovesmatt.com

Contents

BULLETPROOF SETUPS: LEVEL 3 97

Glossary

After-Hours – These are hours after the market closes, during which trading is not open to the general public but a select few. This can cause the price of stock to gap up when the market opens.

Bearish Order – When moving averages are ordered from slowest to fastest, top to bottom. For example, a bearish order could be the 100 moving average on top of the 50 moving average on top of the 10 moving average.

Bullish Order – When moving averages are ordered from fastest to slowest, top to bottom. For example, a bullish order could be the 10 moving average on top of the 50 moving average on top of the 100 moving average.

Bollinger Bands – Bollinger bands show the volatility in a certain stock at any moment; these can also be seen on the stock charts. These bands encapsulate price and expand/contract from volatility. They also are great places to enter or exit trades when prices touch.

Candlestick Patterns – The candlesticks not only tell us what happened that time frame in the market, but they can also tell us what is going on in the big picture. Certain candle formations as well can tell us what exactly will happen tomorrow. Candlesticks are a great place to start learning the market and what the oscillations mean.

Capitulation – This happens at the bottom of selloff or at the top of a bull run and is associated with extreme volume. This is where traders mass liquidate positions at a market top or buy large amounts of shares at the market bottom.

Chopping / Choppy – The movement associated with a market with no direction. This is where the market is range bound and often found to gap up and down consistently. This can be very frustrating for traders trying to nail a direction, but very lucrative for option sellers.

Close – The top of the body of a bullish candle or the bottom of the body of a bearish candle.

Confirmation – This is the exact moment when the trader's bias line up with the market. For example, if a trader thinks that a stock will bounce off a certain price level, he is really guessing until the market gives evidence it will. This evidence of the trader's bias could be that the stock actually starts reversing at that price level. This evidence is called confirmation to the trader.

Consolidation – *Consolidation* is where the market pauses from the direction it has been traveling in. During this pause price is moving up and down, but not really going in a bullish or bearish trend. This *consolidation* can be in the form of a wedge, triangle, or channel. Defined more later in the book. Defined more later in the book in the important terms section.

Day Trader – Someone who enters and exits anything in the market on the same day

Divergence – When the market keeps dropping or popping and the indicator is doing the opposite. This signal tells trader there is likely to be a reversal in the market.

Gaps – (verb) Whenever the market opens higher or lower than where it closed, it produces a gap. A gap can tell a trader a lot whether we will continue higher, fill the gap, and more.

Gaps – (noun) Places in the market where no buying and selling has occurred. Gaps are key pieces of information to understand the market strength or weakness, and there are specific ways to invest and trade from them.

Higher Low – Where the drop of a stock in the market is higher than the previous drop (low).

Long – Where traders believe the market will go up. Being long means, holding positions to profit from this movement higher.

Lower High – Where the pop of a stock in the market is lower than the previous pop (high).

MACD Oscillators – This is another very common indicator that can tell a trader when a trend is reversing or beginning. This indicator has a lot going on, so it is not the easiest for beginning traders, but it certainly is one of the favorites.

Moving Averages – These are lines on the stock market charts that average a certain number of past prices. These are very helpful because they can help users find new support and resistance areas as well as help us gauge current trends. By using these averages, we can learn a lot about the market.

Open – The top of the body of a bearish candle or the bottom of the body of a bullish candle.

Oscillations – This is the act of moving back and forth. For a stock, this could be movements between two different prices. For indicators, this could be movements between two different values.

Oscillators – Types of indicators that move between two values. These indicators could give traders extreme levels for buy or sell signals.

PreMarket – These are hours before the market opens, during which trading is not open to the general public but a select few. This can cause the price of stock to gap up when the market opens.

Price Structure – Amount of buying or selling at certain price levels.

Pullbacks – Short pauses or small reversals. During a large move, or trend in the market, a stock will typically move in the opposite direction shortly after. This short–term move results in a continuation of the trend shortly after. This is how stocks move in a healthy direction.

Retracement – This is a pullback or reversal of a certain percentage. The most popular retracement is 50%. If a stock moves a certain magnitude down, it could reverse half the previous move. Which would be called a 50% retracement. This is ideal for planning profit taking levels.

Risk to Reward – This is where traders find profitability. By planning a trade before hand they can know if it is worthy of taking. This involves knowing what you are risking and what you are trying to make. Any risk to reward above 1:2 preferentially 1:3 is a great set up.

<u>RSI (Relative Strength Index)</u> – One of the most popular indicators. RSI is an oscillator between 0 and 100. Readings around 60–100 are called "overbought" and readings around 0–40 are called "oversold". RSI tells you when the market is a sell or a buy from these extreme readings and is mostly a reversal indicator. Knowing this information can help us enter trades or investments as well as scale–out or exit them.

<u>Scale into A Trade</u> – This is the trading/investing technique for how to properly use position sizes. Scaling is the act of spreading out those orders to achieve the lowest possible average price. You can also scale out of trades, which help you achieve the highest possible exit price.

Smart Money – Money controlled by big banks, institutions, or savvy investors that can manipulate the market because of this amount of money. Traders will regularly follow smart money to ride momentum and avoid getting burned.

Short – Where traders believe the market will go down. Being short means, holding positions to profit from this movement lower. The big concern with being short, is holding short positions, which involve borrowing stock, options, or more. Most brokers will charge a fees for borrowing.

Stop Loss – A place traders will look to exit a position for a loss. This allows traders to avoid larger losses and define how much they are willing to lose in any trade.

Stopped Out – The act of a trader's stop loss getting hit and exiting their position. This can be executed automatically from your broker from an order put in previously.

<u>Straddle</u> – Buying a call option and a put option at the same strike price.

<u>Strangle</u> – Buying a call option and a put option at the different strike prices.

Strong Hands – Shareholders that are quick to hold their shares during any bad news, panic, or fear

Support/Resistance – This is a place in the market where stocks have previously bounced if it happened once in the market, it is likely to happen again. Charting these can give traders/investors great places to enter or exit.

Swing Trader – Someone who enters and exits anything in the market in 1–10 days

Technical Analysis – This is the art of reading stock charts. By analyzing them properly with indicators and patterns, you can get a general edge to help you maximize gains and minimize losses.

Time Frame – Time frames are on a stock chart, just showing the price movement for that time. For example, the 1 minute time frame shows a bunch of 1–minute candles. Each candle represents price movement for one minute in this example. Multiple time frames have different strengths and weaknesses.

Trading Patterns – The stock market gives opportunities for you to draw, triangles, wedges, support, or resistance lines, and with these patterns, you will have the ability to trade or invest from them. For example, if a stock is touching a support line that it has previously bounced off of, that may be a great place to enter a trade.

Trailing Stop Loss– This is where the stop loss rises with the price of the stock. This is a fixed percentage a trader is willing to risk. For example, if the stop loss is set to 5% and the stock rises 10%, the stop loss will be raised to +5%. Meaning the trader will actually lock in positive 5% instead of negative 5%, if the stock reverses.

Triangles – This is a common trading pattern where the stock market may form a triangle. This is a period of consolidation that normally leads to a large breakout.

Volume Profiles – Volume profiles are like daily candle volume but they appear on the horizontally right side of the chart. They can help traders visually see how much buying has occurred at each price level. The more bought, the more resistance or support will be at that price.

Weak Hands – Shareholders that are quick to sell their shares during any bad news, panic, or fear

Wicks – Black lines extending the candle bodies. These indicate weakness in the movement for that candle or trend.

About Market Moves
Matt Giannino

Feel free to skip this part if you don't want to hear how I started trading, I lost it all, quit my job for it, turned accounts from $3,000 to $25,000 multiple times in just a couple of months, teach hundreds how to trade daily, and most importantly found my passion in life. It isn't that exciting.

As you may know, I am or was a professional runner, depending on when you are reading this book. But back in 2016, after my first stress fracture, I used that time to become obsessed with another hobby called Day Trading the Stock Market. For someone working a part-time job that paid very little, this seemed like a dangerous and risky way to spend my free time. I mean, I knew very little to nothing about trading stocks.

One of the main reasons I was attracted to it was a conversation I heard between my Dad and Nick. Back in Boston, after skipping my race that I was too injured to run, they were rambling about the stock market and how everything was beaten up and had plenty of room to run. This amazed me, seeing my Dad and my best friend Nick so excited and passionate about a subject that I heard very little about. Nick was very interested in playing the stock market every day, while my Dad was giving us advice about investing long term. Everything

I heard perked my ears up and moved some rusty gears in my brain. The rest is really history from that day, I dove into stocks and trading with everything I had (literally). This is very common for me; I have an all in or not in mentality. With all this new free time, I was especially all-in now that I could not run and had to find other ways to make my time productive. Running has really let me down lately, and now is the time to increase my knowledge or skills somewhere else. Always keep growing is my mantra, and if you stop growing, you are dying. It is basically science, I mean what else is the point of this life than to make the most of it. Become a better person every day and consistently throw ourselves into the depths of change. That is what I did.

That cold winter in 2016, I spent almost all my time watching CNBC, going to Barnes and Nobles, reading books, and waiting for myself to heal. It was a dark and wonderful time. I started trading with $3,000. For the first 90 days, I would not have to pay trading fees, so luckily, I was really experimenting in the market. During that time, the market was going up every day, and I could only buy stocks, so I felt like a genius. My portfolio was up 50% easily in the first couple of weeks. How could I not be good at trading when stocks rocketed higher every day. I mean, they were coming off very low levels and finally popping. The fact that I could only go long made it easier for me to make money. Obviously this was not enough; having this early success, I wanted to learn more. I stumbled upon options trading not long after being in the market. Which is possibly one of the riskiest ways to trade the stock market, most options expire (or become) worthless. Which means there were unlimited

ways to lose money. But I loved the fact that I could gain leverage from them. If I picked a trade properly instead of making 3%, I could make 80-100%. Why would I not take the options trade? If you guess it, it did not take long before my impressive gains withered away to nothing. Literally nothing, I ended up losing everything in my portfolio, trading those options. Of course, I did, because I had no rules, no structure. The market has no structure. If you mix those things with no structure, it is bound to end in a total financial loss. So I took some time and rethought my strategy. I tried to understand how much more money I could risk in the market, and then I dove back in.

I just got a couple of paychecks and took a week's breather from trading. I realized my mistakes with these foreign derivatives called option trading and moved on. I think now is the time to restart and try again. Not long after that the same thing happened, I stumbled hard and sent another account to zero. Amazing. During this time of healing my injured body, I am also subjecting myself to financial losses. It was miserable, but I went back to the library and the internet to learn more and more and more. I knew the long term benefit of understanding the stock market, and I didn't want to give up on it. I mean tons of people owe 80,000$ in student loans. I just paid $4,000 to the university of trading. It seemed like a cheaper education, in my opinion. One day, I may have $50,000 or even $1,000,000, and at that point, I may see my portfolio swinging $4,000 a day. Long term, I saw the light, I saw the possibility. I knew that this was chump change compared to what I was going to be doing in the future. So that justified using this money to learning. Money really doesn't mean anything; life is short. I don't want to put much emphasis on being rich. I just want to develop skills, especially skills that can make me financially free.

This has already been a long ramble on my back story to trading. Fast forward to 2019, and everything has changed, everything! Good and bad. I spent the next three years trading the markets on and off. On and off, meaning that I would lose everything, I wait a couple weeks or months, deposit some more, and try again. I attempted trading the markets many many times. Options were really really hard. If you had poor risk management, which I had, it was almost impossible to keep any streak going. 2017 ended with a huge loss on my tax return. 2018 started on a bad note but ended much differently. Obviously my negative momentum in 2017 to 2018 led me to lose some money early in 2018. But once I started investing in the summer in stocks and crypto, everything changed. I started my portfolio out with $12,000, and months later, I found it at $25,000. This return was unreal to me, and my options strategy and crypto strategy was finally working. It felt amazing, and I was really killing it. I was so confident that I found the strategy and my purpose or passion in life, I finally quit my part-time job. This was where I taught after-school engineering class and got paid 40 bucks a day. It took about 3 hours, and I had to manage 10-20 kids playing. This was also my third year with the company, and it was time for a change. I just want to say that I had an amazing time meeting all these co-workers, the job gave me the ultimate freedom (I rarely saw my boss, I was my own boss), and I really did it as a means to give back my knowledge of engineering to kids. 90% of the time, I tried to pour my soul into those classes. Helping those kids learn, be more confident in themselves, and have fun, most importantly. It taught me about teaching people, interacting with kids, and being comfortable managing people. These skills will help me out in 2018-2019 just wait (full circle).

So my confidence in trading and investing led me to quit, buy a huge TV as a monitor, and try full-time trading from home. Yeah, I bet you are cringing right now. It seemed like the universe was leading me, so I listened and followed. The signs were there honestly. Not to mention that right before I quit, I shorted the overall market for the first time right before the biggest pullback in 10 years. Yeah, again, confidence was high....too high. So ended up day trading from home for the first month. In the back of my mind, I knew that this freedom was a little too dangerous, and if not appropriately managed would be bad for me.

The big reason I could trade and have more freedom was that if my account is above $25k, I am allowed to trade AS MUCH AS I WANT. Sorry to not mention that part, so that extra freedom was what I was talking about when I said I need to balance it properly. But like I said before, I have no risk management and no rules. I am still bound to fail in the long run, according to most trading books I read. So all this change and being able to make unlimited trades was also coupled with trying to trade futures. This basically was like starting a fire at the gas stations. I was bound to blow up in the worst way. So futures are a derivative different from options in the sense that your losses are not limited, which means that you could lose way more than you put in. If you think this sounds awful, you are right. Oh yeah, I also didn't mention that because the market dropped the largest amount in the last ten years, this jacked up the volatility to insane levels. This means that you make a lot of money quickly and lose a lot of money quickly. These levels were 1 to 3% moves a day in the index when the average was only under 0.3%. It was the most dangerous time to be investing in futures. But I went right in as I do and tried to learn the good and bad lessons first hand. The first couple of days, good momentum carried my account to 28k. And shortly after that, my account dropped below 25k, which is the threshold you need to have to trade as much as you can. So that was tough and added some pressure to trade my way back above 25k. The market was climbing day by day, and I was holding onto my two futures positions, losing thousands of dollars.

I would wake up every day, and it kept rising. My account was slowly shrinking and under 15k at this point. I was fully expecting the market to drop hard and enter a bear market, the super bear market everyone has been waiting for, but it didn't. Just when I sold all my positions to cut my losses and ended the bleeding, my account was at 13k. Which was almost half of what it was when I started. This was too devastating, so I vowed to stay away from futures and decided to take a break. Shortly after I sold, the market did sell off a large amount, the move I was waiting for. If I held everything, my account would have jumped to 50k. Letting me learn the most obvious lesson, right after you sell, is when your move happens. This happens all the time. During this time of trading, I became a little too obsessed, and it definitely took away from my running. I would not be able to sleep if I held any positions overnight, which cuts down on recovery from training obviously. During this time, I still managed to run a 3:43 1500m and a 1:52 800m personal record in track. Oh yeah, you probably forgot that I was still professionally running, and actually healthy now. So I still could balance both, but I would be lying if I said trading didn't take a toll on running in some way or another.

Fast forward one more time to the latter half of 2018 after getting married. During this time, I started a youtube channel that grew to more than 1,000 subscribers enough to get paid by youtube daily. I can attribute this idea and success to Gary Vee. He is an online influencer who preaches putting content on the internet (DOCUMENTING), which is what I am doing. So I listened to him, and now I have one form of passive income and slowly adding more social channels. My goal is to eventually be an online trading influencer, sharing my skills and trades daily. I started trading on Robinhood because it was a free platform where plenty of millennials went to invest. The youtube search was through the rough for Robinhood videos. It was crazy. So I went to this platform just to dabble in investing and show others how to trade.

Only a month later do I buy options to put on TLRY, while it is climbing to 300 and then in the flash of an eye drops to 150$. It was crazy that I was involved in the most profitable day trade in history, I would say, and I was buying this at the exact top. This jacked up my 3,000$ account up to $12,000. It was mind-blowing. The momentum from that led me to get my account to $25,000. Once again, over the day trading limit. Now I was back in business, and I could trade full time again — no more restrictions.

The freedom was back...but could I handle it? This, in the meantime, was all live on youtube, the trades, and the progress. I was displaying it to the world. I would wake up and show my users how to make $1,000 in 15 minutes. I made a $3k to $50k challenge on youtube and slowly brought my account to $46k!! Every day I woke up, I kept making money, and I saw my account grow in a way I didn't think was possible. I was in the zone. At some points trading, I would stretch a little too far and lose a significant portion, like 5-7k. And have to put myself back in check and be smarter. Then one day, I hit 46k, and I wanted nothing more than to hit 50k in front of all my viewers and complete the challenge. From getting married, running fast, getting my account to 25k twice in one year (almost to 50k), creating a youtube channel, personal brand, and more. It has been wild.

Nowadays, what I spend most of my time on is trading, a big surprise. I also post content on youtube every week, teaching traders everything they need to know, as well as offering free courses on my website. I also learned a valuable lesson after making $40,000 in 2 months, that money without people is lonely. It sucks. That is why I share my options trades and setups with a premium trading group every week. This is the best of all worlds; I can trade, teach, and connect with some amazing people. I would love to buy you seven days into my group, no cost for you.

Just click the link here: https://www.marketmovesmatt.com/trade-alert-special

The Power of This Book

If you read my backstory, you may have figured out I spent way too many hours staring at a computer screen watching candlesticks tick up and down. Many people would have given up after going through what I went through, but not me. I never gave up, and I entered the University of Trading every single day of the week. Paid my tuition, learned my lessons, you name it. During these crazy years and 10,000+ hours, I noticed the way the market moves that not many people could ever see. This is where you come in, every pattern, trick, consistency, I saw is logged in this book. These patterns, I learned the hard way, and if I knew them when I first started, my account would be looking a lot different. I put in the screen time till my eyes watered to find secrets in the market that I want to give to you. These are going to be in the form of the very finest setups I have ever spotted trading the stock market professionally for 10,000+ hours. I hope you understand the value and potential of this book, and I hope you take it seriously.

Tips to Success

Study the Book

Here is the thing, this book has setups that I have found to work time and time again. For any new trader, you will read this book, see the setups, and maybe only remember one or two when the market is actually moving in real-time. That is okay! These setups took me years to actually spot instantly charting or trading. The only way you will be able to spot these instantly is by keeping this book by your computer or nightstand and pulling it out every night. The whole goal is cementing these charts in your brain, so when the market moves, it is almost like second nature to say "Double bottom" let's get in on channel breakdown; let's play the drop! Great things take time. Just think about a baseball player hitting a fastball in a split second. They didn't get that ability overnight; it took years of training their hand-eye coordination, reaction time, and form. This book is your training and will help you react faster and more intelligently. This won't happen if you read this once and put it down. Training takes years, and if you want to be good at trading, you need to be consistent and do the hard things.

Ride Momentum and Nailing Pullbacks

You will notice a common theme throughout the book, and you may be shocked by how similar all the setups really are. This isn't because I am trying to rip you off or fill the pages; this is because successful traders understand two things riding momentum and nailing *pullbacks*. You can only make money when you have direction, but once the market chooses a direction, what do you do? Get in right away? Probably not, you may get in on false move or at the very moment the move is over. What the best traders all over the world do with market direction is nail the *pullback*. It is tricky, part science, part art. That is what most of these setups attempt to do, help you nail *pullbacks* at a micro-level for a macro move. The worst way to trade is trying to call the exact moment a lengthy trend dies and the market reverses. Every trader since the beginning of time feels this is a good strategy. This produces menial gains for the trader, compared to trading with the large trend. That is why there are only a few reversal setups in this book. The majority of these setups are just different ways of getting into *pullbacks* in the market, different ways of spotting them, and different circumstances for them. So again, if you feel like all the setups look similar, it is because the concept is, but the details are different. Remember, the devil is in the details.

Flip the Book Upside Down

All setups and plays in this book will only show one direction, a possible pullback or reversal, and either a continuation in that direction or formation of a new trend. You need to understand that all of these setups and directions can be reversed for the exact opposite scenario. For example, many stocks will show the "W Bottom" pattern before reversing. As this book goes over the "W Bottom," you will learn how it leads to a bullish trend after bottoming twice. This can also be found in the opposite scenario, called the "M Top" or double top, where the stock makes two tops in the market and creates a bearish trend. So this one setup can be used in two different scenarios only if you basically inverse everything involved with the scenario. Flipping the book upside down to see the chart inverted is the best way to achieve this perspective.

Another example is an ascending channel, how you can play the breakout or breakdown and channel *resistance/support*. You can do the very same thing with a descending channel. It takes some mental effort to flip all the criteria or outcomes, but I am sure it will make more sense after going through the whole book.

Entering a Trade

All of the setups in this book will contain guidance on how to enter. In some setups there will be multiple places to enter, one risky and one safe. There is one reason why it is important to know the risky entry point. Simply put it may produce more profit, so in some cases it may be worth entering there. These risky entries into trades are only for well-seasoned traders who can manage the risk. The risk involved is a less probable place for the trader to profit and an increased chance of getting *stopped out*.

We Need A Strong Trend

All of these plays, with few exceptions, require a very strong trend to find consistent success. The reason is simple if the trend is truly strong with the momentum, you will find a large *pullback*, long *consolidations*, and a high likelihood, and the trend will continue. Basically, you get a more predictable and sizable movement within the stock. This increases your risk to reward ratio and helps you be more profitable long term. The reason this is true is that if strong trends mean larger moves, traders can make more and risk less with any setup. That is how traders stay in the game the longest by always risking a small amount to make a large return. You may try and use these plays on lower time frames with smaller weaker trends but just know the chance of success greatly diminishes.

Have an Exit Plan

It can't be said enough that when trading the stock market, you need an exit plan. I am not talking about the mouth-watering profit zone, and how many Lamborghinis you will buy when the stock goes there. This is what too many traders do, romanticize the win, and rarely think about the downside. The downside is just as likely to happen as the upside is. So I urge everyone reading this book to plan your trade correctly, which includes a *stop loss* with a profit zone. I just want to make it known that these setups won't help you avoid losses for the rest of the time. Instead, these setups should help you hopefully take less losses over time, but more importantly, to recognize common real-time patterns.

Setting a Stop Loss

Throughout the book this line will be used when referring to a *stop loss*, *"The amount traders risk is fully dependent on how much they think they can make."* When planning out a trade, traders will have an idea of how much they can make. For example, they may believe they can make 10%. Knowing this can make it very easy to figure out how much to risk in a trade. Most traders use a risk to reward around 1:2 or 1:3. The higher the risk to reward, the higher the likelihood a trader will be profitable in the long term. Using simple math, if a trader plans on making 10%, they can risk 3-5% depending on the risk reward ratio chosen. This will greatly help plan how much to risk in any one setup.

Time Frames

The key to indicators, patterns, setups, and all technical analysis aspects is using the correct time frame. Or at least having the right expectations for the time frame you may be trading. The general rule and expectation are that the larger time frames you use, the more accurate and consistent technical analysis will be. This means that most of these setups will become less and less accurate, the lower the time frame. The reasoning behind this is simple; if you are looking at the monthly chart, one candle represents 30 days of price movement and volume. You can make the argument that the monthly candle has 30 times more volume than the daily candle, that means a lot. You can also make the argument that a pattern on the monthly time frame or setup on that time frame, is 30 times more likely to move as expected. If a daily candlestick setup had a 1 to 300 chance of moving as expected, the monthly time frame might have a 1 to 10 chance of moving as expected. I hope this opens your eyes to the power of the higher time frames as well as the dangers of the lower time frames. As you move lower and lower, you have less volume and are subject to volatility more easily. So my point is to know the time frame and the expectation and be prepared for less accuracy on the lower time frames for these setups.

Don't Expect Success

Like any tool in life, it may have amazing capabilities and huge potential, but if you don't know the technique, you won't see the fruits of your labor. The same thing with the skills you learn in the stock market and technique just comes down to execution and emotional control. Any setup you learn in this book might have the potential to be a clear winner all the time, but that is only 50% of the equation for success. The other half comes down to entering the trade, exiting, added to the position, taking off, honoring your stop loss, or profit zone. As you can see, the problem generally doesn't lie in setup but really lies with your choices. Execution is a make or break for a trader, but I am not here to scare you away from trading. My main goal is to provide you with every edge you can possibly have. If the equation for success is setups and execution, then taking the setups out of the equation will make your job much easier. If you can perfect your execution there is no doubt in my mind you can move the markets like a magician.

Important Terms

I am going to go ahead and define the most important terms in this book. If you don't read these terms and fully understand them, this book might be another language. So please, just know these terms before diving into the setups.

Trend

We will be discussing this term in every single setup. A trend is simply a time in the market where the stock is continually moving in one direction. A bullish trend is one where the market keeps making new highs, AKA going higher. A bearish trend is one where the market keeps making new lows, AKA going lower. The more highs or lows the market makes, the stronger the trend. Like going up a flight of stairs, one step at a time, you go higher and higher.

Consolidation

This is another term we will be discussing in every single setup. *Consolidation* is where the market pauses from the direction it has been traveling in. During this pause price is moving up and down, but not really going in a bullish or bearish trend. This *consolidation* can be in the form of a wedge, triangle, or channel. This is a period where buyers and sellers are battling for control, and the result is a bearish or bullish trend. This can be seen in the chart above by the channel that has defined *support* and *resistance*. During this time, the market has no direction and is trying to figure out which direction it wants to go. *Consolidation* periods shortly follow a trending period. Like the example above, the first *consolidation* period was after by a bull run, and the second one was followed by a sell-off. It is hard to know which direction it will be, but with the right setups in the book and clues, you should have a better idea.

Reversal or Pullback

A reversal is exactly what it sounds like, a point in the market where direction changes instantly. For this book, we are only talking about large reversals. Which could be the end of trends or small *pullbacks* from a trend. The difference between a *pullback* and a reversal, is a *pullback* is temporary and allows traders to enter the trend. While a reversal is most likely the end of the trend for some time. *Reversals* last long and become a new trend for the stock. While *pullbacks* are short-lived and can be missed in a blink in some instances. For a bullish trend, a reason for a *pullback* would be an increase in selling pressure or a decrease in buying pressure. Some reasons for this increase in selling pressure could be news driven (Trump tweeting), many sell orders at key price levels (ie. $10, $100, $1000), uncertainty for investors, technical resistance (ie. moving averages), or etc. Obviously most stocks go up over the long haul (5-10 years), so unless the stock has bad fundamentals, the overall direction is always bullish, which means all drops are just *pullback*.

Breakdown or Breakout

The market will develop key levels or patterns that could be in the form of a triangle, channel, wedge, and more. If price breaks higher (from these patterns), we call it a breakout, and if price breaks lower, we call it a breakdown. Just be aware when you go through the setups in the book. Breakouts or breakdowns are the start of a new trend for the market. If you can figure out how the play them quickly, you could be the first to any long move in the market. In the example above, we have two places price broke through, and the subtleties are just in the direction. Simple! The power of a breakout is huge for traders. Coincidently, a false breakout is where the stock looks to pass through that arbitrary place but doesn't (fake out). This is the bane of many traders' existence.

Spotting Key Candlesticks

Again I want to make this very clear; playing reversals is risky, and the best traders will always go with the momentum. The best way to go with momentum is to find an opportune place to buy a *pullback*. The good news is *pullbacks*, *consolidations*, and even *reversals* may show themselves in the same way. Meaning for a trader to have confirmation to enter a trade, they are really looking for the same thing. This is going to be a candle similar to the ones above. All of these candles are seen in the situations listed, and actually give traders greater confidence in those situations. These candles share a couple of things in common. One, they all have *wicks* on the top and bottom; the length is not that important. Two, they all have small bodies relative to the size of the *wicks*. These two facts are important because this indicates a battle between the buyers and sellers, most importantly, indecision. This indecision leads to *reversals*, *pullbacks*, and *consolidation*. Again, *consolidation* and *pullbacks* are opportunities to enter trends. In this book, you will see these candles in almost every setup, memorize them, and put them into context.

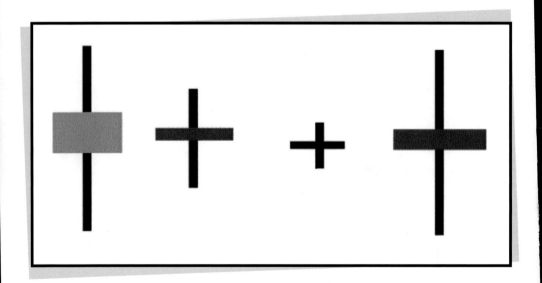

Bulletproof Setups
LEVEL 1

Gap Fill or Bounce

1

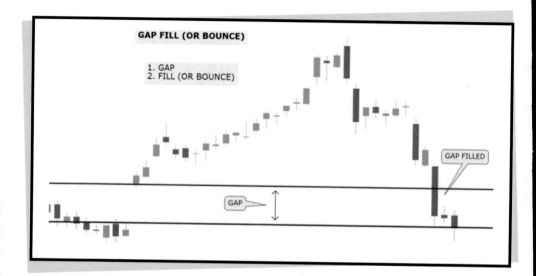

GAP FILL (OR BOUNCE)

1. GAP
2. FILL (OR BOUNCE)

GAP FILLED

GAP

Setup Explained

A gap in the market allows traders to play the filling of the gap or reversals before the gap. The criteria for this setup is simple; you just need to identify a gap, and a stock that is heading towards it. The goal is for the stock to break the first horizontal *support* line that initiates the gap fill. Once that line is broken, the gap fill can happen relatively quickly, and that is where traders can profit.

Why it works

Gaps are formed by the stock being moved during the pre market or after market hours. The reason for these movements could be related to earnings, news, or some other catalyst. When the market opens the very next day, this

MATT GIANNINO

can produce a gap between the *close* of the previous day and the open of the current day. *Gaps* are places with no buyers or sellers (during market hours), and when price heads towards a gap, it will move very quickly through it because of that fact. Simply put, if no buying or selling happened before at those levels, why would it happen in the future.

Warnings

This does not work perfectly because sometimes buyers or sellers will defend levels right before the gap begins (top horizontal black line above); in that scenario, it is best to play the failure to fill the gap, which results in a bounce and reversal off the *support* line. More importantly, it is best to wait for *confirmation*, which is when price enters the gap (which can be seen in the picture below at the point labeled "*long* entry").

Pro Tips

The best place to take profit is at the end of the gap (bottom black horizontal line above) or first price level before the gap began. *Gaps* have a very high chance of being filled, and this is just a healthy movement in the market. Studies have been done that show 91.4% (Bioequity.com) of *gaps* eventually get filled, which tells the power of the gap fill strategy.

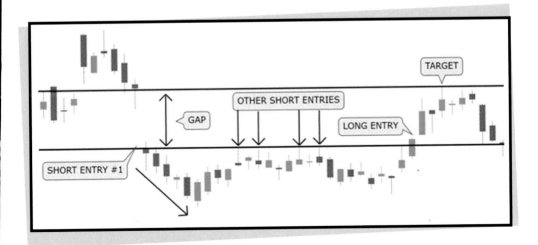

Short Entries

Once the stock *gaps*, there will be a moment where traders will wait to see if it fills the gap instantly or continues in the direction of the gap. The black bottom line defines this place. After the first candle forms, traders may take the *short* side and place their stop loss around the open of that first red candle (*short* entry #1). This scenario plays momentum.

Long Entries

As you can see above, the black bottom line defines where the gap begins. Once price enters the gap, we usually see a move to the top of the gap. This is where traders will usually take profit.

Stop Losses

The stop loss should be placed below (*long* positions) or above (*short* positions) the bottom black line. The amount traders risk is fully dependent on how much they think they can make.

Where to Take Profit

Traders should look to take profit gradually for the gap and go scenario. This is because once the gap forms and the seller keeps pushing it, the stock is usually overextended and cannot go much lower for technical reasons. When this happens, it is best to take profit as momentum slows. This slowing of momentum can be seen by smaller candle bodies and larger wicks, or failure to move higher at the same speed. In the gap and fill scenario, it is best to take profit when the gap fills.

Engulfing Candle Momentum Play

2

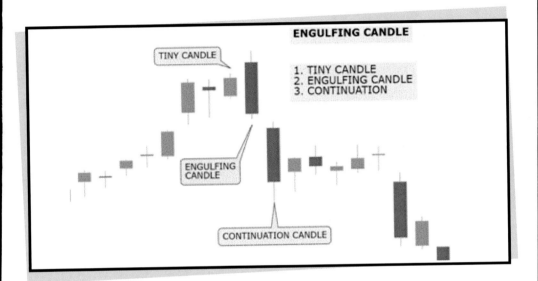

ENGULFING CANDLE

TINY CANDLE

1. TINY CANDLE
2. ENGULFING CANDLE
3. CONTINUATION

ENGULFING CANDLE

CONTINUATION CANDLE

Setup Explained

An engulfing candle is when the market produces a candle where the previous candle is inside the range of the new candle. This candle will 'engulf' the previous candle's body. Think of a Pac-man or Russian nest doll scenario. This is basically the inverse of an inside candle, which is where the market produces a candle where the body is smaller than the previous and inside the range. When we see an engulfing candle, it is very typical that a trend begins and is followed by at least one other candle in the same direction, as seen by the continuation candle above.

Why it works

The psychology behind the levels a candle develops is precious; for example, the tiny candle (above) has an open and *close*. They are very important levels for the future. For the next candle to basically smash those levels moving in one direction, that says a lot about who is in charge in the market. This is a powerful move, that is why we see a continuation with it.

Warnings

In a market with no direction, we see these engulfing candles very often without any continuation.

Pro-Tips

You may not have to wait for the engulfing candle to close to enter the trade. For example, if the candle has already begun to 'engulf,' and there is still time left, it may be good to play the momentum right away as these candles typically close at the lows. There is no telling when it will stop moving in that one direction, and this just increases your risk to reward. Not to mention that you don't have to figure out when to enter on the next candle. You also avoid the scenario where the stock gaps down, and you completely miss the move.

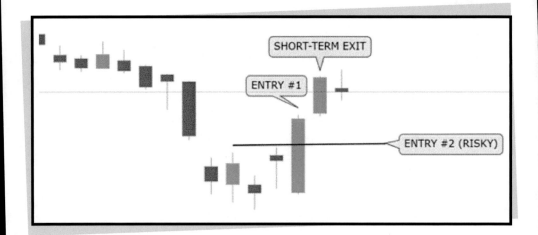

Where to Enter

There are two places a trader can go *long* in this scenario. As you can see, the green candle completely engulfs the red candle. This momentum should bring us higher fast. The better entry point will be at the end of the engulfing candle or the start of the next candle (entry #1). The riskiest entry is going to be right when the first green candle passes the highs of the previous red candle (entry #2).

Where to Place Stop

For this place, your stop-loss is best no lower than ⅓ the candle body. This gives enough wiggle room not to get *stopped out* prematurely.

Where to Take Profit

In this play the trailing stop loss works the best. A trailing stop loss is where the stop loss rises with the price of the stock. This is a fixed percentage a trader is willing to risk. For example, if the stop loss is set to 5% and the stock rises 10%, the stop loss will be raised to +5%. Meaning the trader will actually lock in positive 5% instead of negative 5%, if the stock reverses. This allows you to ride the momentum; however, far it goes, while locking in profit if it reverses.

Continuation Off Open

3

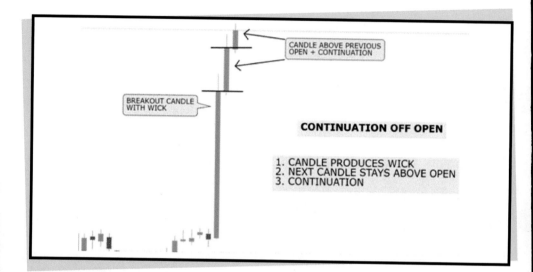

Setup Explained

When you see a trend beginning with a massive candle (like the first green one above), the trend will likely continue on the very next candle. If the price stays above the *close* (or the black bottom line drawn above), you will see the momentum continue the very next day. As you can see from the example above, this happens one more time on the next candle.

Why it works

When a larger candle appears (like the first large green candle), compared to the size of the past candles, it tells us the trend has begun. Like most setups in this book, if traders miss out, they have to grab the *pullback*. This is exactly what the first large candle does before the time ends in the candle;

sellers came in and pushed the price down. That was the *pullback* traders were looking for. If this trend is strong and has more steam, the next candle won't explore much lower than the *close* of the previous candle (black support line above). From there, price should rocket higher for as long as the trend lasts, which is exactly what happens for the very next two candles.

Warnings

The place where the candle closes is key, as drawn by the black lines above. That was the pullback for the trend; therefore, if we see the next candle drop more, it is likely the trend is over or at least losing steam.

Pro-Tips

Most traders will enter these trades after the breakout candle closes, and place a tight stop with a little wiggle room around the level the previous candle closed. You may get *stopped out* doing this, but if it is a true strong trend, the price will not explore lower. This setup is best used on a larger time frame because it is easier to handle the entry, exit, and stop loss. On smaller time frames, 3 candles can move quickly, and if you aren't strategic your stop loss will get triggered (*stopped out*).

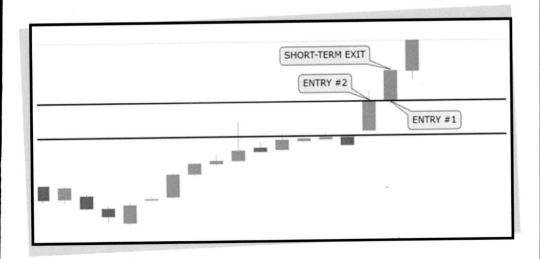

Where to Enter

Once traders find a large bullish candle (with or without a wick), they will then look to enter a trade at the open of the next candle (as indicated by entry #1). This is the best place because the *close* of the previous candle gives traders a defined place to set a stop loss. If the stock ends up gapping higher, this will ruin the risk to reward ratio and make the set up hard to take. Another possible place to enter this setup to avoid gapping is at the *close* of the first bullish candle (entry #2).

Where to Place Stop

The stop loss should be placed below the *close* of the first bullish candle (or below the open of the entry candle). The amount that traders risk is fully dependent on how much they think they can make.

Where to Take Profit

This play the trailing stop loss works the best. This allows you to ride the momentum; however, far it goes, while locking in profit if it reverses. It is hard to have a defined profit target since the trend could go forever.

Channel Support or Resistance Bounces

4

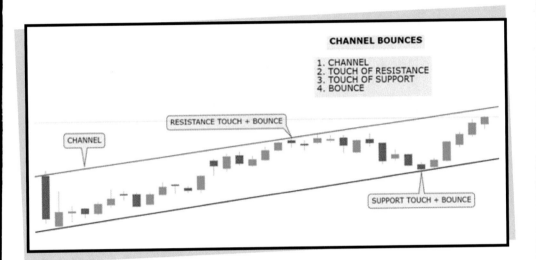

CHANNEL BOUNCES

1. CHANNEL
2. TOUCH OF RESISTANCE
3. TOUCH OF SUPPORT
4. BOUNCE

RESISTANCE TOUCH + BOUNCE

CHANNEL

SUPPORT TOUCH + BOUNCE

Setup Explained

A channel, whether ascending, descending, or flat, is a perfect place for traders to play the *oscillations* in the market. The key to a channel is spotting it early as you can, to play the up / down movements as many times as possible.

Why it works

These lines that arbitrarily develop in the market are called supply and demand lines. So whenever prices get close to the *support* (demand) line, we see buyers come in, and likewise, when the price gets to the *resistance* (supply) line, we see sellers come in.

Warnings

The channels work very well initially, but the longer they trade inside the channel, the higher the chance we see a breakout. So your confidence should be high that it will hold in the beginning, which is usually the first 2-3 touches to the *support* and *resistance*.

Pro-Tips

The key to drawing a channel as early as possible, in the example above, is to draw the trendline at the first *resistance* (i.e., *resistance* touch+bounce above) and connect it to the prior *resistance*. Then, using the slope of that line, make another trendline connecting to the lowest point of all the candles. The first line will be the top *resistance* line of the channel, and the second line will be the *support* line of the channel. That second trendline would have helped you predict the *support* touch + bounce before it actually happened. Traders never know if a channel will hold, but some key signs are very high or very low relative volume and smaller candles.

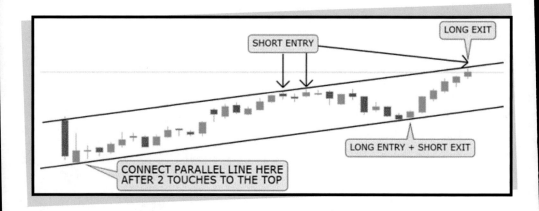

Where to Enter

The best place to enter *short* is touches on the top of the channel (*short* entry). The best place to enter *long* is touches of the bottom (*long* entry). The bottom can easily be defined once we have two touches to the top. Just take a parallel line and attach it to the lowest part of the channel. This will help predict future bottoms before they happen.

Where to Place Stop

The stop loss should be placed below support or above resistance lines. The amount that traders risk is fully dependent on how much they think they can make.

Where to Take Profit

The most common place to take profit for *short* positions is the bottom of the channel (*long* entry + *short* exit) and the top of the channel for *long* positions (*long* exit + *short* entry). It is also common to take profit halfway down the channel.

Bulletproof Setups
LEVEL 2

Post Trend Pullback Pops

5

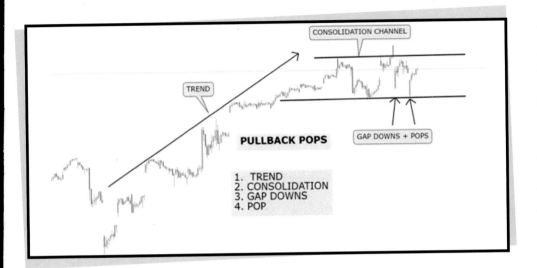

Setup Explained

After a trend in the market, there will always be *consolidation* shortly after. In the setup above, the *consolidation* channel was quickly found when the stock made a defined high (black top line) and sold off to a defined low (black bottom line). This can be seen above by the *consolidation* channel lines. At the height of the trend where the *pullback* begins, we can chart the top *resistance* line of the channel, and the *support* line can be drawn at the first true bounce. *Chopping* (the movement associated with a directionless market) is the single worst thing that can happen to a trader if they don't recognize it. It is very frustrating and can lead to continuous losses. This is because one hour something is going up, the next hour it is going down, and repeat that for multiple days. During these moments, when the stock *gaps* down near support, we end up seeing aggressive buying ONLY if the trend was initially bullish. In the example above, this actually happened two times in a row where the stock gapped down and instantly was bought up and rose the whole day.

Why it works

Pullbacks do not last long after a strong trend in the market. Especially once the stock starts consolidating. Once the channel is developed during *consolidation*, big banks with a lot of capital, will move the market in some shocking ways. The channel is a gift for traders if they can recognize it early, and what normally happens during these periods is gapping in the stock market. Meaning, big banks will move the stock pre or post-market to cause fear and panic in an attempt to scare weak shareholders (*weak hands*). This allows "*smart money*", as we call it, to buy the shares from *weak hands* for a discount. For example, in the chart above, we see two gap downs in the stock. During this time, *weak hands* start selling to big money, and this is why the stock runs aggressively. In a strong trend, most people wish they got in earlier, so whenever the stock drops, they use it as an opportunity to get in at a lower price finally. When you think about big banks constantly buying the dips as well as those who missed out buying, there is consistent buying pressure throughout the consolidation of the channel. The momentum from a strong trend lasts long and we see waves of buying at discounts.

Warnings

Buying the first *pullbacks* in any trend can be very, very nerve-racking. This is extremely hard to do mentally, but just knowing that you are playing the long term trend. The best way to calm your nerves is to gather other pieces of evidence of the reversal or continuation in the trend.

Pro-Tips

As you can see in the chart above, the stock touched a channel *support* level multiple times. This level was found on the very first *pullback* in the market and held for the future. This just gives the trader an extra reason to buy the *pullback*, because now it is sitting on *support*. There are other pieces of evidence you can use to grab these *pullbacks* with confidence, which could be a *bollinger band* touch or a moving average touch. All of these could have helped increase your confidence and evidence for seeing a reversal.

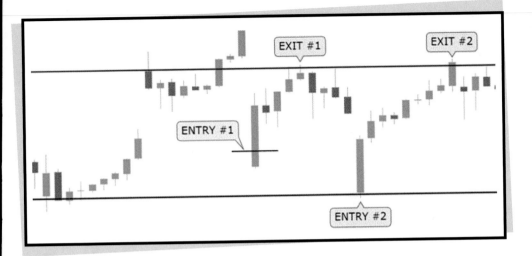

Where to Enter

During a strong market, pullbacks (gap downs) don't last long. The best place to enter the first gap down is right after the market reverses (entry #1). Once price starts moving higher from the open, traders can ride the momentum and place their stop at the low of the day. For entry #2, we have a defined *support* level. This gives us extra evidence we will reverse. BONUS: At the blak top line of channel *resistance*, where traders take profit (exit #1/2), that could also be a place to enter a *short* position.

Where to Place Stop

The stop loss should be placed below *support* for entry #2 and below the open for entry #1. The amount that traders risk is fully dependent on how much they think they can make.

Where to Take Profit

The optimal place to take profit in a channel is at *resistance* or *support*.

W BOTTOM

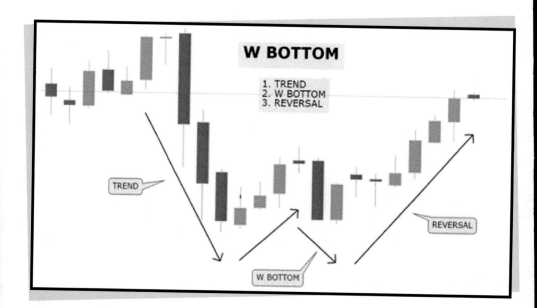

6

Setup Explained

In a trend in the market, you may see a quick reversal (or bottom), followed by another move in the direction of the trend. The best time to enter any reversal trade is at the double bottom. These bottoms usually lead to long term reversals and changes in the trend.

Why it works

A trend is typically only strong if it continues, so in the example above, the first reversal higher off the trend showed weakness in the overall trend. Traders have learned time and time again that nothing bottoms once in the market before completely reversing and making a new trend. What we normally see

MATT GIANNINO

is a second bottom (where the W bottom call-out is pointing), whether it is an equal touch of the previous bottoming levels or a *higher low*. There is no science behind why stocks bottom twice before changing the trend. It could be that big banks need more time to accumulate; the stock hits *resistance* on the first small reversal or many other factors. But the truth is, the W bottom (or the double bottom) is a powerful pattern that leads to a strong move.

Warnings

Timing the bottom of a move is never easy and can lead to a lot of pain. Most traders never try to catch a falling knife. This is because you never know when the bottom is in, so be very careful trying to get into a double bottom too early.

Pro-Tips

The double bottom may lowest the stock may be for a long time. Once the bottom is confirmed and price starts reversing, you want to be in that trend as quickly as possible. Another place to enter that offers less risk are the two *consolidation* candles following the reversal. These candles are next to the reversal call-out box, and the *wicks* were great evidence these candles represent *consolidation* instead of reversal candles. Overall great evidence that the stock will continue higher. As a trader, the goal is to enter a trend during *consolidation*.

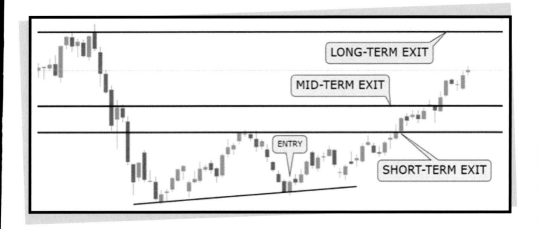

Where to Enter

The key to entering the W bottom is waiting for *confirmation* that it will defend the previous low made on the first bottom. The green candle (entry) on the double bottom gives traders *confirmation* of this pattern. The double bottom can be tricky to enter. Because looking at the example above, the stock actually doesn't make it to the exact previous bottom. Most traders will buy the first green candle (entry), or bottoming candle on the second bottom. At that point, you can draw a trendline like the example above.

Where to Place Stop

The stop loss should be placed below *support* or above *resistance* lines. The amount that traders risk is fully dependent on how much they think they can make.

Where to Take Profit

Short term traders will take profit in the middle of the W *resistance* (highest point between the two bottoms). Swing traders will take profit around the 50% *retracement* of the previous downtrend. This also lines up with a previous *consolidation* zone, as seen in the example above by the 3 candles. The long term traders will hold this until the new trend retraces 100% of the previous downtrend.

MACD Buy or Sell Signal

7

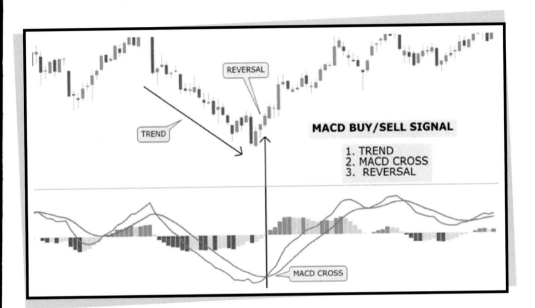

Setup Explained

The MACD cross is one of the simplest buy/sell indicator signals. The main strategy for playing the MACD is to look for a large trend, and the two moving averages can also confirm this on the MACD below. The larger the move, the greater the gap between the moving averages. This represents the magnitude of the trend, and when we have a strong trend the MACD will work the best. Towards the end of the trend we see the faster moving average cross, the slower; this initiates a buy signal. This also happened to be the very bottom of the trend and the exact reversal point for a brand new trend. The MACD is brilliant at spotting reversals with a very clear signal. The MACD can be played in a variety of other ways but this is the most common and accurate signal from this indicator.

Why it works

Just like one of our other setups, the moving average crossover, this is exactly the same. Just played two moving averages and how they move with one another. When the faster-moving average is on top of the slower, that means we are in a bullish trend, and when the slower moving average is on the top faster, that means we are in a bearish trend. The reason we need a strong trend for this to work really well is that it produces a very large reversal. When stocks move in extreme ways, they also reverse in extreme ways.

Warnings

Indicators historically produce false signals, basically if you took a trade every time these lines crossed, you would be broke tomorrow. Again, this is just another piece of evidence that should be used only if all the right circumstances are met. For example, later in the stock chart, the MACD almost crosses and eventually crosses shortly after that. The reversal at that moment is weak and would not have produced large enough returns relative to the risk. This is most likely due to the MACD almost crossing, that moment weakened the possible move to the downside when it actually crosses later. You will see this happen a lot with the MACD, where you think you are going to get a perfect cross and it just doesn't.

Pro-Tips

It only makes sense from a risk to reward standpoint to only trade a clear crossover in the MACD. It is very important to develop a plan for a stop loss because like I said previously the MACD is historic for producing false signals. Also, here are some MACD pro tips. Traders will also only take bullish positions when the two moving averages are above the zero line which is where the histogram flips (basically the middle of the MACD). As well as only take bearish positions when the moving averages are below the zero line. On the chart above, this proves to be 100% true as the stock only moves higher in the bullish trend when it is above the zero line and only moves lower in a bearish trend when it is below the zero line.

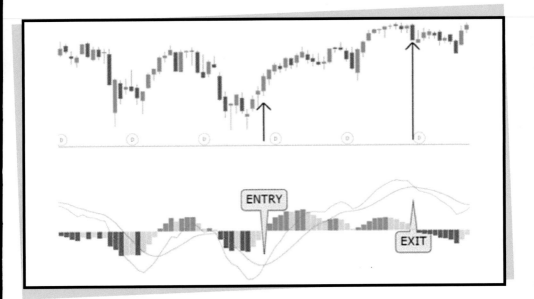

Where to Enter

Best *long* entry is when the MACD moving averages cross, fast over slow (like the entry above). Best *short* entry is when the MACD moving averages cross, slow over fast (like the exit above).

Where to Place Stop

The MACD is hard to figure out where to put the stop loss. But just like the other examples, it can be placed a certain percentage lower than the entry point. The amount that traders risk is fully dependent on how much they think they can make.

Where to Take Profit

The best place to take profit from *longs* is when the MACD is moving averages cross again, slow over fast (like the exit above). The best place to take profit from shorts is when the MACD moving averages cross again, fast over slow (like the entry above).

Bottom Bollinger Band Pullback

8

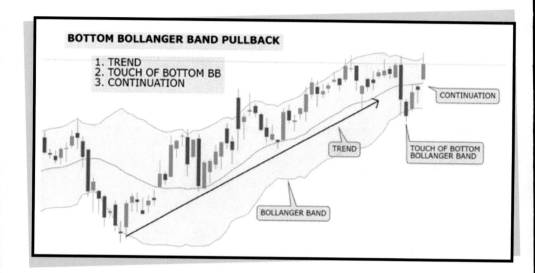

BOTTOM BOLLANGER BAND PULLBACK

1. TREND
2. TOUCH OF BOTTOM BB
3. CONTINUATION

CONTINUATION

TREND

TOUCH OF BOTTOM BOLLANGER BAND

BOLLANGER BAND

Setup Explained

During a trend, the candlesticks will normally only stay within the upper *bollinger band* and the midline. In a real strong trend it will rarely go under the midline. Usually, at the end of the trend, before we begin consolidation, the first real sell-off will touch the bottom *bollinger band* almost perfectly. Once price touches the bottom *bollinger band* the sell off usually comes to an end. Traders see this time and time again; this is a healthy test of the bottom of the *bollinger band* and usually leads to a quick bounce and continuation to prior highs as seen in the chart above.

Why it works

As we have seen throughout this book, trends don't reverse instantly. What they normally do is *pullback* and then continue in the direction of the initial trend, or possibly start consolidating. As traders, we are just looking for the right place to enter these trends, and this type of *pullback* is most likely gold. The reason the stock consistently bounces off the bottom *bollinger band* on the first big sell off is that *bollinger bands* represent where the price can possibly go at any given moment. It expands and contracts due to volatility. From past price movements, *bollinger bands* attempt to predict future price movements, although it is not always 100% accurate it gives us a visual idea of how far price can travel. So once we get that *pullback* to the bottom *bollinger band*, that is the extent of how far price could have traveled down. In theory, it is the best place to enter for bounce and continuation in the trend.

Warnings

On any *pullback*, it can be dangerous entering. It is just hard to know if it is actually the bottom when the stock touches the bottom *bollinger band*. As you can see in the example above, the stock first touched the *bollinger band* and produced a wick, and the very next day continued lower before finally reversing/bottoming out. If you bought on the first touch and saw the stock drift lower the next day, you may have been confused and frustrated. This is because you bought too early, you didn't have *confirmation* of the actual bottom. Be patient; it pays!

Pro-Tips

The safest way to play this move is to wait for actual *confirmation* that the stock has bottomed and is heading to the mid *bollinger band*. The evidence for this bottom could be irregular volume, a gap up the next day (like the example above), indicator *confirmation*, a certain candlestick pattern, candlesticks with wicks, or more. The trick to playing *pullbacks* is placing a stop loss at the lowest part of the move, with some wiggle room.

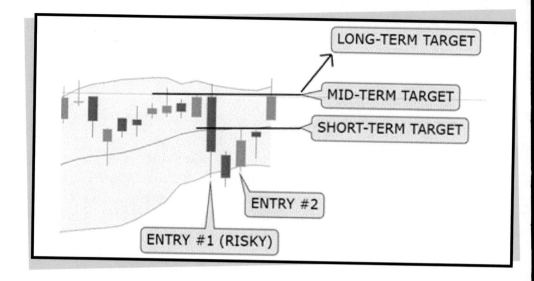

Where to Enter

This is a very hard set up to enter. The risky entry point will be at the first *bollinger band* touch (entry #1), but there is no promise that it bottoms there. The better entry point is when the stock spots making new lows (entry #2). This could be seen by a gap up, bottoming candle, green candle, or more.

Where to Place Stop

The stop loss should be placed below *support* or above *resistance* lines. The amount traders risk is fully dependent on how much they think they can make.

Where to Take Profit

The best short-term target is the mid *bollinger band* or the 50% *retracement* of the prior move. The mid-term target is the previous highs or 100% *retracement* of the preceding move. The long-term target would be a continuation of the trend until it gets weak.

Cup and Handle

9

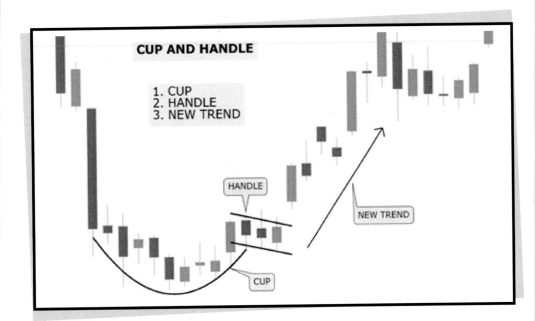

CUP AND HANDLE

1. CUP
2. HANDLE
3. NEW TREND

HANDLE

NEW TREND

CUP

Setup Explained

The cup and handle pattern is a bottoming and reversal play. The criteria for this usually include an initial trend, followed by *consolidation* (in the form of a cup), small breakout higher, followed by a flag(handle), and finally, the start of a new long term trend. This pattern can be tough to spot, but when you do, it can be a very profitable play.

Why it works

The trend slowly dies in the cup portion of this setup. This can be seen by the stock trying to go lower, but each move lower is not as far the drops before.

These failed attempts to really drop mean buyers are holding up the stock; this intense battle between the buyers and sellers leads to the reverse. Now the stock starts popping, but every drop is higher than the last. This shows the buyers are slowly taking control by moving the stock higher. This brings us to the end of the cup pattern, where the buyers take quick control before the handle. The battle isn't over here because the buyers and sellers go at it again, now producing a handle or a flag. This is seen as a pause in the buying and usually leads to a massive move, which is exactly what happens in the example above. The story of this pattern is basically the slow and methodical battle as the bulls overtake the bears. Victory is shown in the new trend after this pattern.

Warnings

This is a tough pattern to spot in real-time. Not the mention very complex and involves almost a perfect fit of the cup and handle. The key is to try not and force it if the cup and/or handle doesn't look or fit perfectly. It might be best to move on instead of imposing some idea of what will happen to the stock.

Pro-Tips

The larger the cup, the larger the breakout. Most stocks after a severe sell-off will take months to actually bottom. This is fine; this just means that big banks wants to accumulate shares at cheap prices quietly. During these long extended bottoms in the market, it will be much easier to chart, spot, and trade this pattern. Traders may never see a handle form on the chart to enter, and that is okay. This setup is very bullish with or without the handle on the chart.

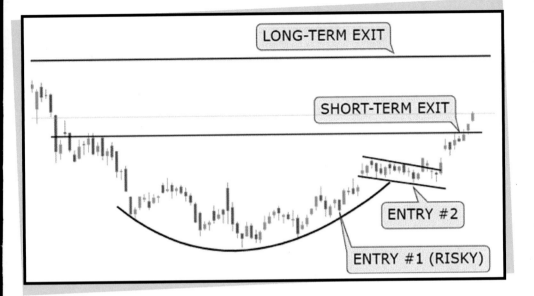

Where to Enter

Traders will look to enter this setup at the upper portion of the cup (entry #1). This will act as *support* and will shortly be followed by the first breakout. The next less risky place to enter is at *support* during the handle *consolidation* (entry #2). This *consolidation* is short and likely followed by the larger move. This *consolidation* will come in the form of a wedge or descending channel.

Where to Place Stop

The stop loss should be placed below the cup support arc (entry #1) or the *consolidation* support line (entry #2). The amount that traders risk is fully dependent on how much they think they can make.

Where to Take Profit

Traders should look to take profit at prior *consolidation* levels for a short-term exit. The best long term exit is at the full *retracement* of the preceding move.

High Volume Node Profit Zone

10

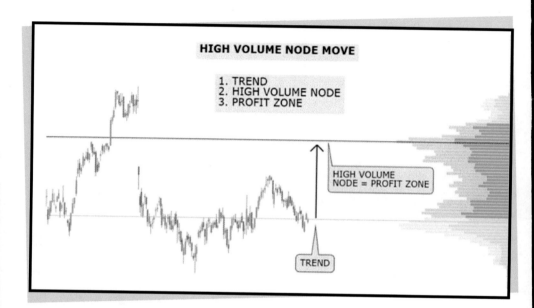

Setup Explained

On the right side of the chart you may see a possible mountain range. The peaks are called high volume nodes, which also look like bell shaped curves. High volume nodes are places for *support/resistance* as well as good places to use for profit zones. In the setup above, the stock has the potential to make a run higher, but will quickly run into the high volume node. At this point, it is smart to use this place to take profit, as it requires tremendous volume to move through this zone.

Why it works

Volume profiles, which are depicted above, show volume from a horizontal point of view. All this tells traders is how much volume is bought at every price level. It is quite a genius. In theory, if a lot of volumes were bought at a certain price (let's say $61), then buyers and sellers will come back to that level to defend it. The larger the volume profile bar goes out, the more volume that was traded there, meaning the harder it will be to break through it. In the real world, this could be similar to the fact that avocados are either $1.00 or $2.00. Nobody wants to sell or buy avocados for $1.50, but the two previous prices produce a lot more buying and selling for some reason.

Warnings

A high volume node is a bell-shaped curve, and at the peak, the highest volume bar is usually the best place for *resistance* or *support*. As you can see above, the rounded bell-shaped curve that is a high volume node makes this idea of *resistance* or *support* vague. The worst part is, if you zoom in on the screen or out, the high volume node will completely change. This, unfortunately, is a very general zone where we don't know exactly where the price will stop. When price moves towards the high volume node it may not exactly touch the highest volume profile, it could stop short or move through it slightly before reversing. This is the one big problem with this indicator.

Pro-Tips

These are great for getting more details on a current trade but not great for planning trades. Like I said before, it is really hard to predict how the price will react around these zones. If you are already in a trade, it may give you extra evidence to know why the price is pausing or why it is moving fast. The best traders will make a note of these levels but not be married to them. These also can be used on every single candle as important levels for day traders, but I don't have nearly enough pages in this book to explain that.

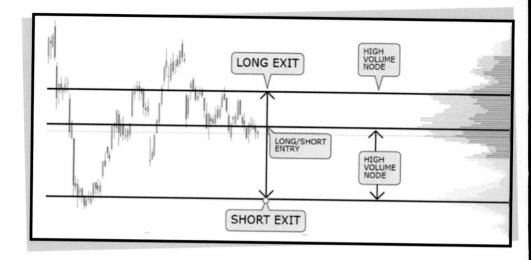

Where to Enter

High volume nodes provide traders with excellent places to enter trades. If the price is below the high volume node, it will be a good *short* entry and above will be a good *long* entry.

Where to Place Stop

The stop loss should be placed below support or above resistance lines. The amount that traders risk is fully dependent on how much they think they can make.

Where to Take Profit

After traders enter a trend, they will look to take profit at the peak of a high volume node (defined by the lines above).

Short Squeeze End of Trend or Reversal

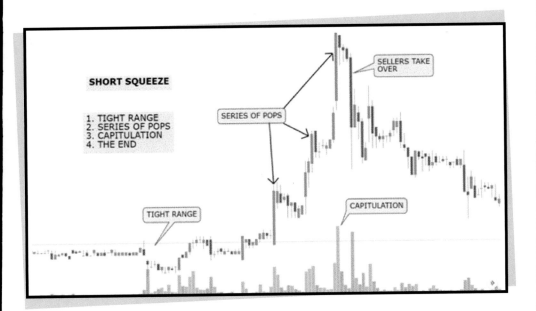

11

SHORT SQUEEZE

1. TIGHT RANGE
2. SERIES OF POPS
3. CAPITULATION
4. THE END

SELLERS TAKE OVER

SERIES OF POPS

TIGHT RANGE

CAPITULATION

Setup Explained

The *short squeeze* setup is pretty simple, the stock starts in a tight range and most likely has been consolidating for months. But all of a sudden, during this consolidation, we start to see some volume pick up despite the stock not really moving. Then as soon as you know it, the stock makes its first pop, then possibly, another, and another. This series of pops can last forever only if the volume stays small. An already insane move will eventually makes its last move, the "*short squeeze*," which can be confirmed by the *capitulation* volume as well as the swift drop after.

Why it works

The *short squeeze* is one of the most aggravating candles for a trader. These are seen in moments where a stock soars to unbelievable levels, and seeing all these people make money really quickly can create FOMO and irrational behavior. Most traders during this time think that the stock can't go any higher, so they *short* it, while those who feel the FOMO start buying it. As the FOMO buyers push up the stock, the shorters take losses, which results in more buying. Then at some point in all of this, we reach capitulation, which is the end of the move. That is where buying ceases, and the stock drops. Then irrational buyers now start selling for a loss, and the shorters come back in full force.

Warnings

Timing the top of a *short squeeze* is only a skill for veteran traders, so be very careful trying to *short* this monster. It may be best just to wait for the capitulation volume, followed by the big selling volume.

Pro-Tips

The *short squeeze* is a way to know the market tops for huge moves easily, but it is just as easy playing the upside before the *short squeeze* even happens. These series of pops could be 100-300% per move depending on the stock, while the downside of a *short squeeze* is only 50-80%. You do the math, which direction makes more sense.

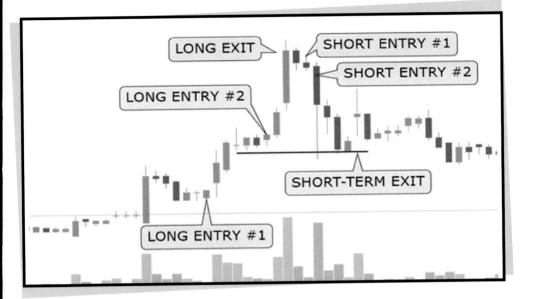

Where to Enter

Before the *short squeeze* happens, traders can play the momentum and try to enter at *consolidation* zones (*long* entry #1+2). Once the *short squeeze* is confirmed, usually by volume, the best entry is at the first bearish candle. As you can see from the example above, there is an aggressive entry #1 and safer entry #2.

Where to Place Stop

When entering *short* positions, traders should place their stop loss above the prior highs. The amount that traders risk is fully dependent on how much they think they can make.

Where to Take Profit

The best exit for *long* positions if playing the momentum is when volume starts to double or triple for the time frame the trader is watching. With large upwards movements and abnormal volume, this is usually the sign that the *short squeeze* is coming to a climax. The best short-term exit for a *short* position is the first consolidation zone of the prior move. The long-term exit is going to be a 100% *retracement* of the preceding move.

Resistance / Support Rejection

12

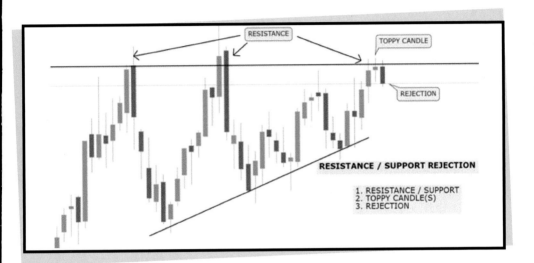

Setup Explained

When we have a predefined *resistance* or *support* level from the past, it tends to be huge *resistance* or *support* for the future. As we see in the example above, the price touched this level three times, and on the third time, we are presented with a toppy candle. The basis of a toppy candle is one with a thin body and *wicks*, especially above the *resistance*. The more candles like this we see at *resistance* or *support*, the better. At this point, we look for rejection and reversal.

Why it works

These *resistance* or *support* levels that were developed in the past gives us evidence where buyers or sellers were interested and most likely will be interested again. For example, this resistance level (in the chart above) was a place where sellers wouldn't let price get above, so they consistently put their sell orders at this level. This can be visually seen by the *wicks*.

Warnings

The more times price touches a resistance or *support* level, the higher chance that it will breakdown, because eventually sellers/buyers dry up. Just like *chopping* a tree, you never know when the tree finally gives out and falls. The same thing with *resistance* and *support* levels, we just don't know when the next touch will push it completely through. The other downside of playing these rejections is that we never know how far it will pull back from the *resistance* or *support*.

Pro-Tips

The typical rule is on the third touch of an important level; we usually see a follow-through that level. So looking at the example above, price did reject it in the short term, but it could very well breakthrough higher later.

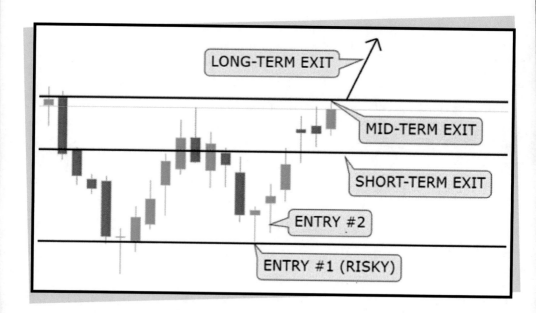

Where to Enter

The risky entry for this trade would be the first touch of the *support* line (entry #1). The safer entry for this trade would be the actual rejection of the *support* (entry #2). As you can see in the example above, this can be seen by the wick making a higher low and moving higher the next couple candles.

Where to Place Stop

The stop loss should be placed below *support* or above *resistance* lines. The amount that traders risk is fully dependent on how much they think they can make.

Where to Take Profit

The best short-term exit is the first consolidation zone or 50% *retracement* of the prior move. The mid-term exit is going to be a 100% *retracement* of the preceding move. The long-term exit may be a break to new highs and a continuation of the trend.

Failed Moving Average Breakthrough

13

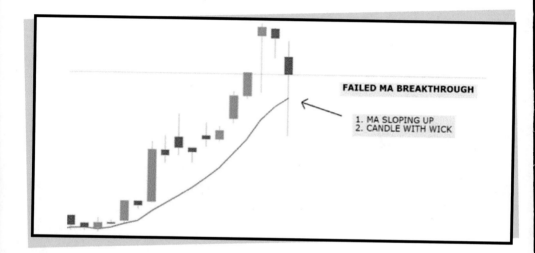

FAILED MA BREAKTHROUGH

1. MA SLOPING UP
2. CANDLE WITH WICK

Setup Explained

When we see a moving average that is sloping upwards with a trend in the market, any *pullback* through the moving average will most likely fail. Looking at the picture above, at one point, the candle had a full red body that cut right through the moving average. This usually doesn't last; at this moment, traders will likely play the reversal as the candle usually closes above moving averages sloping up.

Why it works

We see this all the time in the market, the stock is trending in a direction and makes a *pullback* to a fast-moving average sloping straight up. During these *pullback* times, the reversal rarely lasts long. This is because of two factors, first, the price cannot easily cut through a moving average sloping straight up, second, for stock to truly reverse the fast-moving average generally needs to be flat or sloping down.

Warnings

Not much to say here, this goes with the universal saying, "Don't fight the tape." So if you are trying to go against the trend, that fast-moving average may smack your bank account.

Pro-Tips

These are great opportunities to get into and play the long term trend. These *pullbacks* to the ten moving average end up being the "coulda, shoulda, woulda" scenarios. Meaning you might look back ten days later and wish you got in.

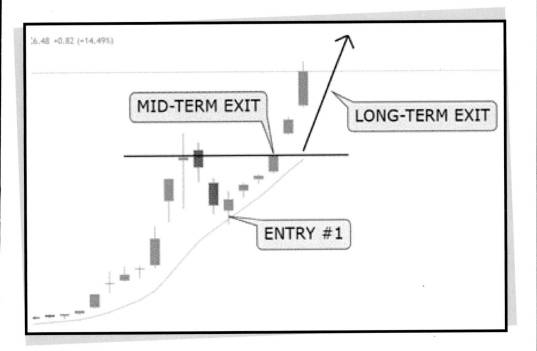

Where to Enter

The risky place to enter is at the break of the ten moving average because price generally doesn't stay below (entry #1). When the candlestick closes on top of the moving average, this will offer traders a safer place to enter, which will be during the very next candle (after entry #1). This confirms the support, and we normally see a bounce shortly after.

Where to Place Stop

The stop loss should be placed below the moving average. The amount that traders risk is fully dependent on how much they think they can make.

Where to Take Profit

This setup is best for day traders as they can place the bounce easily. Profit should be taken just shortly after, while long-term traders can look to exit at the prior highs, hold for a continuation of the trend, or exit with price crosses the ten moving average.

Pennant or Wedge Pullback Breakout

14

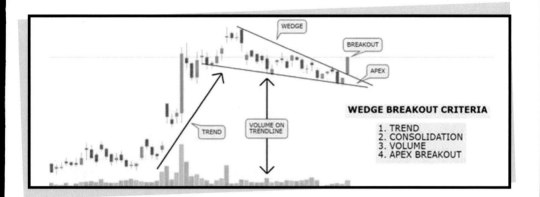

Setup Explained

After a trend is initiated, there is a huge possibility of a *pullback/consolidation* in that trend. This may come in the form or a wedge or pennant (we call it a pennant when the stock pulls back from a trend, wedges usually form when the stock slows down in a trend). As price chops through the defined *support* and *resistance*, we get to a special point called the apex, and this is most likely where we see the breakout and continuation with the trend. As seen in the example above.

Why it works

During every trend, it is very healthy for the stock to *pullback*. During these *pullback* moments, the range gets smaller and smaller, until the apex of the wedge. At this moment, the market just might have removed all the sellers with multiple *pullbacks* and will be able to move higher. This breakout move from the wedge means the trend has fully begun again because all the selling pressure has been removed.

Warnings

At the apex of this pattern, a move can theoretically happen in either direction. We cannot always assume a breakout in the direction of the trend. So don't be married to your plan and instead react to the situation.

Pro-Tips

When the breakout higher happens, most traders will take profit in the middle of the wedge/pennant range or the ultimate high of the initial trend. This is because after consolidating for so long, it is very uncommon for the market to make new highs instantly. The *consolidation* and breakout could just lead to more *consolidation* on the macro level.

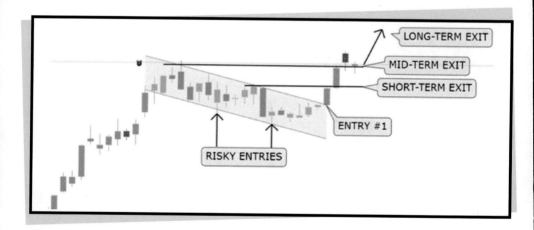

Where to Enter

This setup is best to enter on the *support* touches (risky entries). The only problem is traders cannot expect a breakout, and sometimes waiting can provide the best entry point (entry #1).

MATT GIANNINO

Where to Place Stop

The stop loss should be placed below *support* or above *resistance* lines. The amount that traders risk is fully dependent on how much they think they can make.

Where to Take Profit

The best short-term exit is the first *consolidation* zone or 50% *retracement* of the prior move. The mid-term exit is going to be a 100% *retracement* of the preceding move. The long-term exit may be a break to new highs and a continuation of the trend.

Moving Average Crossover   15

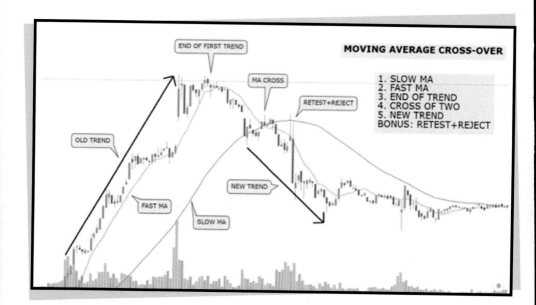

MOVING AVERAGE CROSS-OVER

1. SLOW MA
2. FAST MA
3. END OF TREND
4. CROSS OF TWO
5. NEW TREND
BONUS: RETEST+REJECT

END OF FIRST TREND
MA CROSS
RETEST+REJECT
OLD TREND
NEW TREND
FAST MA
SLOW MA

Setup Explained

After a trend, the market will tend to pull back a healthy amount, and during these times, it may be easy to play the downtrend with a simple moving average crossover. As you can see in the chart above, we have two moving averages, the fast and slow moving average. This could be the 10 MA (moving average) and 50 MA, or the 50 MA and the 200 MA. After the trend comes to an end, the fast-moving average will cross the slow moving average, producing a sell signal. After crossing, more often than not, the market will drop/pop and head into a new short term trend. If you are lucky and didn't enter the trade of the moving average crossover, you will be presented with a golden opportunity to enter the retest and rejection of the moving averages. As you can see in the

MATT GIANNINO

example above, at this point, we produced two candles with large wicks that lead quickly to a move lower. These new trends may not last long; that is why it is important to scale out quickly.

Why it works

Stocks that are trending in one direction typically have moving averages ordered from fastest to slowest (top to bottom) for bullish trends like the example above. But once the fast moving average is underneath the slow-moving average (crossover), now they are stacked for a bearish trend. Moving averages, in general, are *resistance* or *support*, so in the example above, once the price goes below the moving averages after the crossover, they acted as a *resistance*. With the fact that they were stacked in a bearish way, it gives us a high probability of seeing the new trend begin in the opposite direction (selling).

Warnings

Moving average crossovers do not always produce a new trend that is easy to profit from. The crossover may also happen late, meaning the new short term trend may have ended after the signal. Moving averages of all sorts cross every single minute in the market, and if you played them all, you might go broke. Be selective and experiment before jumping on this setup.

Pro-Tips

The key to playing the moving average crossover correctly is to look for a steep trend. The steeper the trend, the more likely the pullback will produce an exciting enough move.

Where to Enter

There are three great places to enter this setup. The first being, once price crosses the ten moving average (*short* entry #1 and #2). The second being, the slow and fast-moving averages cross (*short* entry #3). The third, which doesn't always happen, being the retest and rejection of the moving averages above (*short* entry #4).

Where to Place Stop

The stop loss should be placed above moving average lines. The amount that traders risk is fully dependent on how much they think they can make.

Where to Take Profit

The way traders got in could be the way they get out! Either when the price goes above the ten moving average, when the slow and fast-moving averages cross, or when price retests or rejects the moving averages.

Support or Resistance Level Break and Retest

16

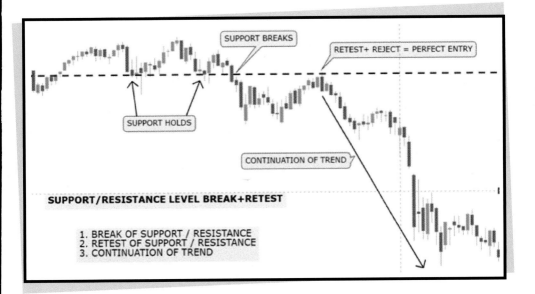

SUPPORT/RESISTANCE LEVEL BREAK+RETEST

1. BREAK OF SUPPORT / RESISTANCE
2. RETEST OF SUPPORT / RESISTANCE
3. CONTINUATION OF TREND

Setup Explained

When the market produces defined *support* and *resistance* levels, it may break and allow profiting from the new trend. As you can see from the example above, the *support* level was defined as it held the price at two separate points. Then all of a sudden, price breaks through the *support* level and doesn't fall much. This is because new trends take time. So the market ends up retesting the new *resistance* level, and at this point, it rejects it. This is the best place to enter any trade. It is at a retest and reject of a predefined level. From there, it continues to lower fast.

Why it works

New trends take a while to develop, especially after breaking a key level, big moves don't always happen instantly. This is very normal after the market has been tight and consolidating for a long time. The market needs time to weed out the buying pressure, turn moving average down, or several other random reasons. We really don't know exactly why these changes in direction take time.

Warnings

When playing breakouts of key levels, you will run into a headache of false breakouts. This is where the market moves through *support* or *resistance*, but it doesn't last long. Very similar to the first breakthrough, the *support* line. As we see above, if the price at the retest+reject zone went higher and never dropped, this would be a classic false breakout. One of the most aggravating moves that can happen to any trader. This is always the risk of playing breakouts. That is why it is key to keep a stop loss on a reversal back through the *support* or *resistance* level.

Pro-Tips

The best place to enter these setups is to get as close as possible to the *support/ resistance* level and keep a firm stop a little higher than it. Just like the chart above, at the retest+reject zone, you could enter a short position and put your stop loss in a small amount above the *resistance* line. This just setups traders up to be apart of the move and help them to get out if a false breakout is going to happen.

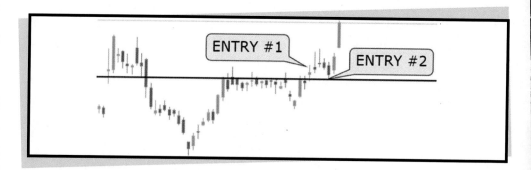

Where to Enter

There are two great places to enter this setup. The first being, once price crosses the *resistance* level (entry #1). The second, which doesn't always happen, being the retest and rejection of the *resistance* level (entry #2).

Where to Place Stop

The stop loss should be placed below support or above *resistance* lines. The amount that traders risk is fully dependent on how much they think they can make.

Where to Take Profit

The best short-term exit is the first consolidation zone or 50% *retracement* of the prior move. The mid-term exit is going to be a 100% *retracement* of the preceding move. The long-term exit may be a break to new highs and a continuation of the trend.

Inside Candle Reversal

17

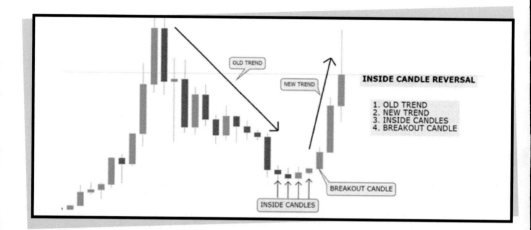

INSIDE CANDLE REVERSAL

1. OLD TREND
2. NEW TREND
3. INSIDE CANDLES
4. BREAKOUT CANDLE

Setup Explained

Inside candles are a great opportunity to play a reversal in a stock. The key to finding this setup is to have a trend slowly die to the point where you see very tiny candles with very tight ranges. The first candle sets the range for the rest to trade within. This is the inside range, and once the stock breaks out from the range, this where the new trend (reversal) begins. As shown in the chart above.

Why it works

Inside candles at the end of a trend signify a place of *consolidation* and a weakening of the trend. In the example above, the bottom of this trend allows big players to accumulate a large amount of stocks from the hands of the desperate shareholders who lost money. In a bearish trend, this is a place where all hope is lost, but the smart money managers know it's an opportunity of a lifetime. They keep the range small because they are quietly buying,

MATT GIANNINO

doing it when nobody expects it. If you can recognize it, you can be apart of the breakout.

Warnings

This doesn't necessarily mean a reversal; the trend could always continue after this. That type of pattern would then be referred to as a flag. So always be prepared just to play to break out from the range, don't be married to the direction.

Pro-Tips

The more inside candles you have, the larger the breakout that occurs shortly after. In this example above, we had four inside candles, and the breakout leads to a massive bull run.

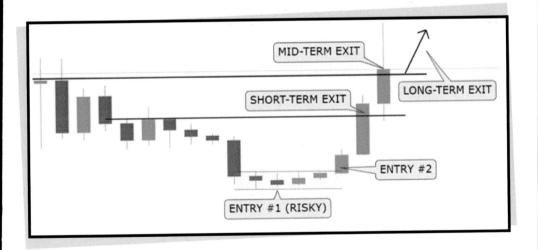

Where to Enter

The risky place to enter this setup is a touch of the *support* level of the inside candles (entry #1). The safer entry will be a confirmed breakout from the *consolidation* zone, and this will lead to a large move (entry #2).

Where to Place Stop

The stop loss should be placed below *support* or above *resistance* lines. The amount that traders risk is fully dependent on how much they think they can make.

Where to Take Profit

The best short-term exit is the first *consolidation* zone or 50% *retracement* of the prior move. The mid-term exit is going to be a 100% *retracement* of the preceding move. The long-term exit may be a break to new highs and a continuation of the trend.

Bollinger Band Squeeze

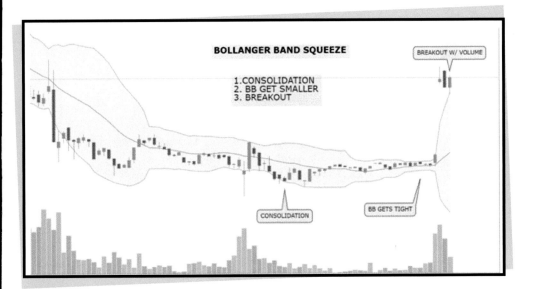

18

BOLLANGER BAND SQUEEZE

1. CONSOLIDATION
2. BB GET SMALLER
3. BREAKOUT

BREAKOUT W/ VOLUME

CONSOLIDATION

BB GETS TIGHT

Setup Explained

During *consolidation*, we see the range get tighter and tighter, making the *bollinger band* get smaller and smaller. Visually the *bollinger band* helps us see this squeeze and allows us to get ready for the move after. As you can see in the example above, the *bollinger band* squeeze leads to a breakout quickly after.

Why it works

A move after a tight range like this is on purpose; it is meant for the big players to trap the smaller players. Think about it; everyone who shorted the scenario above while the stock traded in a tight range was losing during this gap up. Most of these traders, losing the need to cover *short* positions by buying stock, in turn, magnifying this move even more.

Warnings

When the stock gets this quiet, and the range gets tight, the next move could be swift and in any direction. So it can be really dangerous trying to guess before the move happens and can lead to huge losses.

Pro-Tips

After a trend when you see the *consolidation* and the range get this tight, there is a very high chance the stock moves hard or even *gaps* (like the scenario) in the direction of the initial trend. Options traders can make a killing during this time by owning calls and puts, but only if the move happens soon and a certain magnitude.

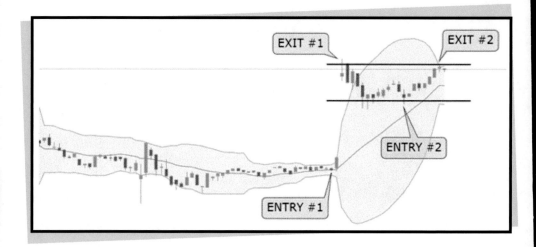

Where to Enter

The risky place to enter this setup is pre breakout. Again because we don't know the direction of the breakout, this can be very risky. The safer place to enter this setup is once price breaks out. But again this can be tough if price *gaps* higher, playing *gaps* is never easy for traders

Where to Place Stop

The stop loss should be placed below support or above *resistance* lines. The amount that traders risk is fully dependent on how much they think they can make.

Where to Take Profit

The best short-term exit is the first consolidation zone or 50% *retracement* of the prior move. The mid-term exit is going to be a 100% *retracement* of the preceding move. The long-term exit may be a break to new highs and a continuation of the trend.

Indicator Divergence and Reversal

19

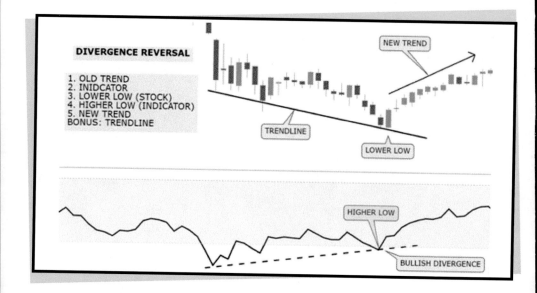

DIVERGENCE REVERSAL

1. OLD TREND
2. INIDCATOR
3. LOWER LOW (STOCK)
4. HIGHER LOW (INDICATOR)
5. NEW TREND
BONUS: TRENDLINE

NEW TREND

TRENDLINE

LOWER LOW

HIGHER LOW

BULLISH DIVERGENCE

Setup Explained

When a stock is trending down and making new lows, but the indicator is making *higher lows*. This means that we could see a reversal in the trend because of the weakness found in the indicator. As you can see in the example above, the trend completely reversed because of these internal factors with the stock.

Why it works

A strong move would consist of the stock making a new low/high and the indicator making a new low/high. If that is not the case, like the example

MATT GIANNINO

above, it indicates weakness in the trend. This weakness can also signal the end of a trend, or the reversal. This is mainly signaling the internal weakness for the stock, whether it be the buyers or sellers starting to struggle.

Warnings

Playing any reversal reading can be dangerous, so that is why it is important only to play extreme readings. Only those will yield the largest reversal move.

Pro-Tips

Other pieces of evidence, like trendlines, can greatly increase your chance for success in this setup. You can use most indicators to spot *divergence*, but one of the favorites is the relative strength index. This is most popular for divergent readings. The indicator above is actually my own, "Market Mover" indicator, which I programmed over the years. Most indicators have big flaws and false readings. I made my own to fix that problem, and it is the only indicator I use today. This indicator is offered to anyone in my trading group for free. More information can be found at http://www.marketmovesmatt.com.

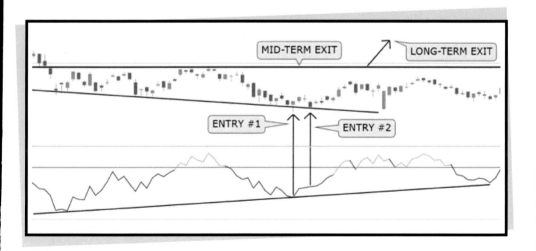

Where to Enter

This setup can be extremely hard to play if traders don't find other evidence of a bounce. For my example above, trendline *support* was used, but without that, it would be tough to know when to get in.

Where to Place Stop

Because entering this setup can be vague and not defined, our stop loss has to be the same. The amount that traders risk is fully dependent on how much they think they can make.

Where to Take Profit

The best short-term exit is the first *consolidation* zone or 50% *retracement* of the prior move. The mid-term exit is going to be a 100% *retracement* of the preceding move. The long-term exit may be a break to new highs and a continuation of the trend.

Head and Shoulders

20

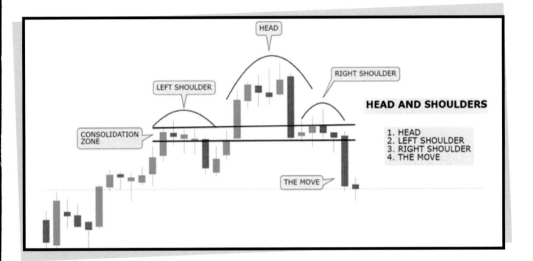

Setup Explained

The head and shoulders pattern above is where we see weakness and eventually breakdown lower. The left shoulder is formed by consolidating and followed by a breakout higher and more *consolidation*. The next *consolidation* level is considered the head. At this point, for whatever reason, the stock may do the reverse of what happened initially. Which drops to the previous *consolidation* range (left shoulder), bounce around some more (right shoulder), and then make one last drop. The last drop is the most predictable and where traders can enter and profit.

Why it works

The first two pops and followed consolidations (left shoulder and head) above are very bullish. But when the market drops back down to the left shoulder region, a new trend has begun. If the trend were truly bullish, there would be no need to explore lower, just the act of dropping means the trend is likely dead. Now at the right shoulder, the sellers can't move through past *consolidation* levels very easily. What we see is a pause right at the same level as the left shoulder. This *consolidation* lasts just as long as the left shoulder, and we usually see a drop shortly after. This is a highly predictable pattern.

Warnings

This pattern is very hard to spot, and even if you do, you may get chopped out before the move. For example, in the right shoulder above, we see the price go above or below the *consolidation* zone (2 black lines). During this *choppy* action, we get faked out both ways, and if you put your stop loss to close, you most likely will take an early loss in a winning play.

Pro-Tips

Look towards the left shoulder to know where to put your stop-loss, look to see how large the false breakouts were (candle *wicks*), this will help you avoid getting stopped out. Mainly by increasing your stop loss above those previous candle *wicks* on the left shoulder.

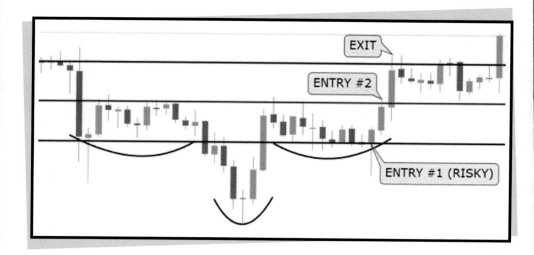

MATT GIANNINO

Where to Enter

The risky place to enter this setup is at the *consolidation* zone. The safer place to enter this setup is at the breakdown of the *consolidation* zone.

Where to Place Stop

The stop loss should be placed below support or above resistance lines. The amount that traders risk is fully dependent on how much they think they can make.

Where to Take Profit

The best short-term exit is the first *consolidation* zone or 50% *retracement* of the prior move. The mid-term exit is going to be a 100% *retracement* of the preceding move. The long-term exit may be a break to new highs and a continuation of the trend.

3 Bar Play

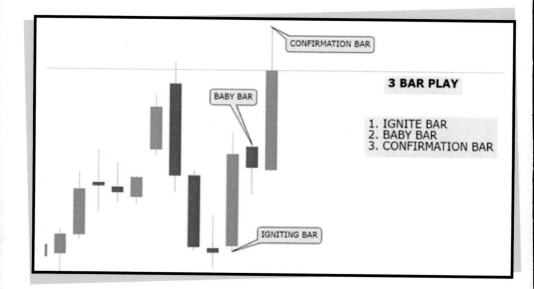

21

Setup Explained

This setup is very simple and just involves 3 bars (candlesticks). The first candlestick is called the igniting bar because it ignites the trend. This candlestick should have a larger body than most previous candlesticks. The very next candle is a gift to all traders; this is a *consolidation* candle or called the baby bar. If the range of the baby bar stays above the top third of the range of the igniting bar, this will setup perfectly for a continuation with the confirmation candle. The baby bar is a gift to all traders. This gives traders a defined level to put their stop loss (at the *close*) and the ability to enter on the trade on the next candle as long as it stays above the *close* of the previous candle. As traders enter on the third candle, all they can do is hope not to get *stopped out* and for a continuation of the trend. There are also two possible places to enter on the third candle, one is at the open and hope for a run-up

MATT GIANNINO

instantly, and two is at a break of the highs of the previous two candles. If all criteria are met with the first two candles, the chances are likely it will continue.

Why it works

This is in line with everything we have learned thus far in the book. Trends begin, and traders look for *pullbacks* to get in. The three-bar play is the perfect setup to do just so. The main reason it works is that the igniting candle has a longer body than the previous candles and may have volume accompanying it. It also works because the *pullback* or consolidation with the baby bar is a very tight range, which shouldn't travel much lower than one third the size of the igniting candle. *Pullbacks* in large moves are completely normal, expected, and healthy. The key is that the next candle holds the lows of the baby bar, and breaks the highs of the baby bar. This is called an engulfing candle, which we learned about earlier in the book. Again, engulfing candles indicate complete strength in the trend. This makes the 3 bar play, one of the easiest plays for new traders.

Warnings

This is a tough setup because every detail has to be in place for it to work out perfectly. Traders have to be aware of the volume as well because an igniting bar without volume is meaningless. The volume will confirm this move and will sustain it long term.

Pro-Tips

This is a play for a quick profit; most traders will take profit at the end of the confirmation candle. The trend will only last if there is a sustained or building volume, as well as new highs.

Where to Enter

The best place to enter this setup is on the third candle after the highs are broken from the two previous candles (entry #1).

Where to Place Stop

The stop loss should be placed below the low of the baby bar. The amount that traders risk is fully dependent on how much they think they can make.

Where to Take Profit

The three-bar play is typically a quick move, which is very helpful for day traders. Although you can ride out this momentum for the longer move, it is typically best for traders before the close of the confirmation candle.

MATT GIANNINO

Copy Cat Candles

22

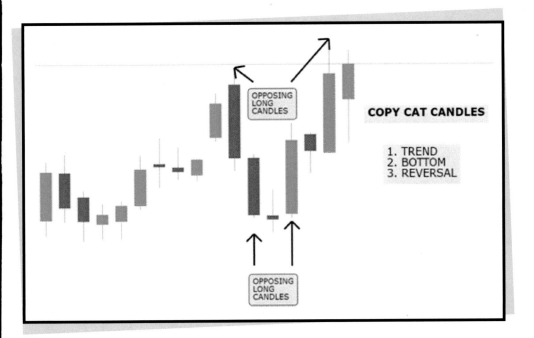

OPPOSING LONG CANDLES

COPY CAT CANDLES

1. TREND
2. BOTTOM
3. REVERSAL

OPPOSING LONG CANDLES

Setup Explained

The key to this setup is spotting a trend that involves very long candles. If these candles dropped quickly on the news, this setup works even better. After the drop from these long candles, we will eventually get a bottom. This can be spotted by the bottoming candles referred to by *"Spotting Key Candles"* earlier in the book. This is a prime place to enter for a reversal because just as quickly as the stock dropped is how fast it could go up.

Why it works

The market may drop aggressively due to news, earnings, Trump tweets, or more. During these times, it is quick and emotional, and there is minimal buying and selling. Just like our bulletproof setup #1, the gap fill, there is little to no buyers or sellers at previous price levels. This poor *price structure* means there is no reason for buyers/sellers to revisit those levels in the future. Looking at the example above, the two candles that dropped may have no structure to them. We can only confirm this by looking at candle volume, or better yet, *volume profiles*. After bottoming and reversing, the next green candle will match the size of the opposing candle only if the *price structure* was weak. Again, if there was small volume and no structure on the sell-off, this will produce a bull run of the same magnitude because of that. This runs true for the next large candle of the reversal, equalling the size of the candle on the first drop.

Warnings

The key to this working effectively is having that large swift candle move in the market. This ensures a poor *price structure* and lets the reversal move happen to the same size as the opposing candle. If for any reason, there was constant buying and selling as the stock fell, it will be much harder for the stock to rise through these price levels again. The main problem with this setup is that a trader cannot expect a swift big candle reversal every time. Only certain market internals for the stock needs to be met and unfortunately, these are invisible to most unless they can analyze *volume profiles*.

Pro-Tips

There is a chance this setup may actually be a gap down in the stock. For example, this could be a weekly candle and one day during the week the stock gapped down. This gap won't be shown on the weekly candles, but only the daily candles and lower. If it actually was a gap down in the stock, we know for sure there was no buying and selling in the candle body. This means that the reversal candle is very likely to be as large as the opposing candle. When entering this trade, it is important to keep a stop loss at the low bottom; a break below the lows will ruin this setup and result in a continuation of the selling.

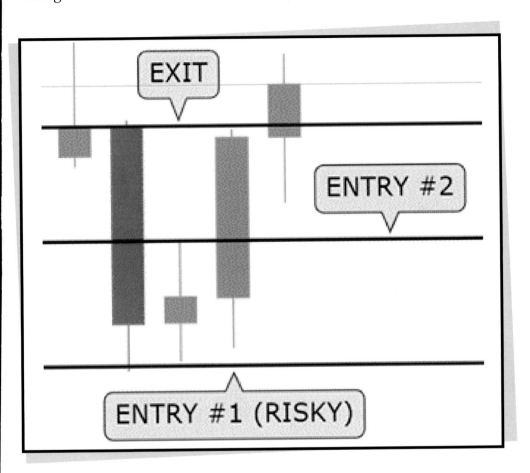

Where to Enter

The key for this play is to enter during a breakout (entry #1). When you see a large opposing candle and price enters the range of that candle, traders usually see an equal move. The riskier place to enter is before the copy cat candle develops at some type of *support* from the bottom (entry #2).

Where to Place Stop

The stop loss should be placed below *support* or above *resistance* lines. The amount that traders risk is fully dependent on how much they think they can make.

Where to Take Profit

The best place to take profit is at the top of the body of the previous copy cat candle. This could be the open or the *close* depending on the direction.

Bulletproof Setups
LEVEL 3

Flat Moving Average Magnets

23

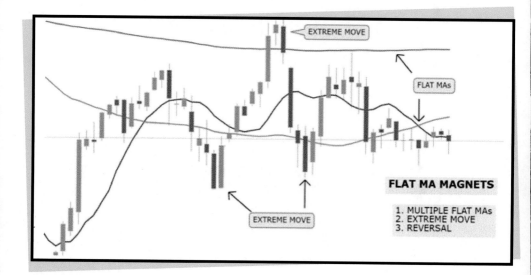

Setup Explained

When you have multiple moving averages on the chart, and those moving averages are all flat/close to each other, extreme moves will likely fall back to the middle of the moving averages. During these times, it is best to play the highs/lows for this trading range or possibly think of selling options.

Why it works

Moving averages represent an average of price, and if they are becoming flat, that means there is no direction in the market. There is this concept of mean reversion, which is basically price reverting to the mean, or the moving

MATT GIANNINO

averages. In the example above, because there are so many moving averages all together, it is really difficult to produce a long term move. During these times, we only end up seeing reversions from the extremes of the range to the moving averages (middle of the range). This can happen for a long time until the moving averages get closer and closer together, then we see a much larger move (similar to bulletproof setup #30). The only way to kick start a new trend is with news or a catalyst.

Warnings

This set up represents a *choppy* (directionless) market, so be careful trading the chop. It is very easy getting stopped out, and you are a slave to any news completely destroying your plan.

Pro-Tips

Try to add another piece of evidence to understand what is happening; this could

be volume, trendlines, *divergence*, or more. This type of market can be very random; that is why it is important to stack more evidence.

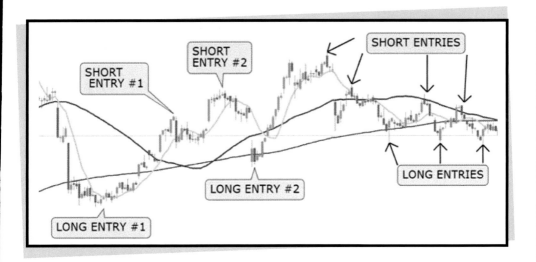

Where to Enter

Once traders see an extreme move away from the moving averages, it is best to enter after a bottoming candle (as talked about in *"Spotting Key Candlesticks"*). For example, when the price dropped under the ALL moving averages (*long* entry #1), we start seeing candles with thin bodies and long wicks. This indicates the momentum is dying and allows traders to play the move back through the moving averages. The *short* entries are above ALL the flat moving averages, and are followed by a large red candle to confirm the reversal (*short* entry #1 and 2). The *long* entries are below ALL the flat moving averages, and are followed by a large green candle to confirm the reversal (*long* entry #1 and 2).

Where to Place Stop

Entering positions in this setup can be vague and not easily defined, our stop loss has to be the same. The amount that traders risk is fully dependent on how much they think they can make.

Where to Take Profit

This is a great setup for short term traders because of the *choppiness*. Movements don't typically last long, and it's hard to tell where price will go. There is no obvious place to take profit in this setup. Traders can take profit when price crosses one, two, or three moving averages. The more moving averages it crosses the longer a trader may need to hold.

Channel Breakout and Fall Back

24

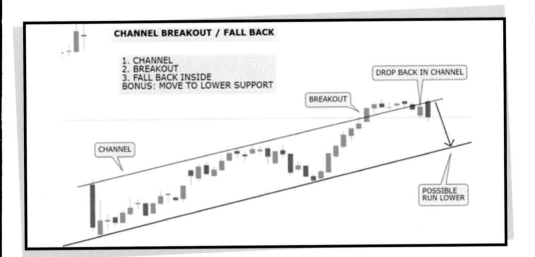

CHANNEL BREAKOUT / FALL BACK

1. CHANNEL
2. BREAKOUT
3. FALL BACK INSIDE
BONUS: MOVE TO LOWER SUPPORT

DROP BACK IN CHANNEL

BREAKOUT

CHANNEL

POSSIBLE RUN LOWER

Setup Explained

This set up works very well with upward trending channels. In these channels, the price may occasionally break out of the channel to the upside. This will not last long and we eventually see a fade back into the channel. The ideal and optimistic target is the bottom of the channel, but sometimes all we may get is the move back inside the channel.

Why it works

In a trend, the size of the move is usually defined by the channel. As said previously, the top line in the channel is pegged with sellers, so a move outside the channel is defying supply and demand. This is a very extreme movement for the stock. Extreme moments in the stock market do not last long, and because of this, we see price fade back into normalization (the channel).

Warnings

When playing a channel in the stock market, you can get *stopped out* with moves like this. If we *short* this stock at channel *resistance* and we break higher, traders see losses. The worst strategy if price is outside the channel and you already lost money, is doubling down. Just because the price may eventually enter the channel again, doesn't mean traders need to double down. Many times when it enters the channel again, it will be higher because the channel is ascending.

Pro-Tips

There are many ways traders play this, they usually play the breakout, play the retest/bounce outside the channel (post breakout), or fade the move back inside the channel. This requires expert-level execution and is not for the faint of heart. Obviously momentum is bullish during a breakout like this, so the best move is just to go with momentum until it disappears.

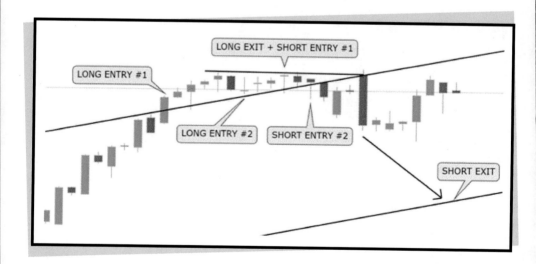

Where to Enter

There are a couple of places to enter this setup. This setup can be played for the bulls and for the bears. The best bullish entry point would be a breakout of the channel (*long* entry #1). Another place could be a touch of the channel *support* after the breakout (*long* entry #2). This could be used to play short-term momentum. For the bearish play, traders will enter *short* positions at the height of the trend outside the channel for a move back inside (*short* entry #1). The second *short* entry is when price enters the channel again.

Where to Place Stop

The stop loss should be placed below *support* or above *resistance* lines. The amount that traders risk is fully dependent on how much they think they can make.

Where to Take Profit

The ideal spot to take profit would be at the bottom of the channel (*short* exit), but sometimes price never makes it that low, Most traders will also take profit in the middle of the channel.

Channel Breakdown and Retest

25

CHANNEL BREAKDOWN + RETEST

1. CHANNEL
2. BREAKDOWN
3. RETEST
4. DROP

RETEST

BREAKDOWN

DROP

CHANNEL

Setup Explained

In an ascending channel, we sometimes see exhaustion, which would be in the form of *lower highs* until we breakdown lower from the channel. How we play this is very different from the bulletproof setup #25 because when we breakdown lower out of a channel price may never enter the channel again. Like we pointed out earlier the channel is continuously going up, and if price is going down, it becomes harder and harder for them to meet again. This type of play is for *pullbacks* or the start of a reversal trend, and the best place to enter is a retest of the channel (like the example above). As you can see in the example above, the first breakdown didn't start the bearish trend, but the retest + rejection of the channel was the beginning of a long term sell-off. Traders can make money on the initial channel breakdown, but it is always safer from a risk to reward standpoint to enter on the next sell off (channel retest+rejection).

MATT GIANNINO

Why it works

Channels represent two lines where buyers and sellers have historically defended. For the bottom channel *support* line to give out, that means that buyers are no longer interested and have stopped defending it. Now that buyers are weak, the sellers basically have full control. Like we said earlier in this book, it takes a while for the trend to reverse, and because of this, we usually see breakouts or breakdowns followed by *chopping*. This is healthy and offers traders an ideal entry point. Which is when price touches the channel *resistance* line (bottom black line) and rejects it. This will ignite a large sell off and give traders the ideal place for entry.

Warnings

This retest may never happen, meaning the first move outside the channel may be the only opportunity to enter.

Pro-Tips

Don't ever try to predict moves outside of the channel; just try and react when they happen. More often than not, the price stays inside the channel for extended periods.

Where to Enter

One place to enter this setup is a the break of the channel (entry #1). A safer entry, that doesn't always provide itself to traders, is the retest/rejection of the channel (entry #2).

Where to Place Stop

The stop loss should be placed below the channel *support* line. The amount that traders risk is fully dependent on how much they think they can make.

Where to Take Profit

The best short-term exit is the first *consolidation* zone or 50% *retracement* of the prior move. The mid-term exit is going to be a 100% *retracement* of the preceding move. The long-term exit may be a break to new highs and a continuation of the trend.

Moving Average and Bollinger Band Squeeze

26

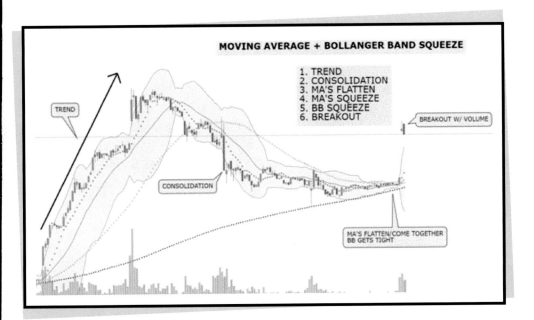

Setup Explained

Like most good setups in this book, this setup requires a trend and *consolidation*. This *consolidation* is a little different and requires two important indicators, *bollinger band* and 2-3 moving averages (i.e., 10-yellow, 50-blue, 100-red). These indicators give us two important signs that the trend will begin again; firstly, the moving averages basically come together almost touching and flatten out (or slightly sloping up is a bonus). These moving averages must never slope down together; this is going to be huge support for the stock during the *pullback*. The next indicator that really matters is the *bollinger band*. During this consolidation, the *bollinger band* will squeeze, getting smaller and smaller. Possibly to the point where they almost touch, like the example above. At this point, we are experiencing the penultimate squeeze for a breakout, and the stock is bound to move hard. Which is exactly what happens in this example, we see the stock actually gap higher.

Why it works

During a *consolidation* from a trend, this a smart move from big players to trap the smaller ones. The *consolidation* may cause traders to get excited and *short* the stock for the downside. But as the buying pressure eventually comes back, the stocks rip higher quickly, during market hours or after hours to gap the stock. This will trap all sellers at that moment and they will be forced to buy, to cover shorts pushing the stock higher faster. This *consolidation* above shows almost no volume. This means the buying pressure has taken a break and <u>does not</u> mean the selling pressure has increased. This is a key difference found by reading the volume. The buyers are paused until big news comes out or some other catalyst.

Warnings

As the example above proves, the stock gets really quiet, and it is not known when it will actually move higher. There is no correct formula to predict the timing. Just know when it does move, it will move fast or gap up, making it extremely hard to get into the move. If the stock *gaps* higher, you have to act instantly with a vague plan of your stop loss and profit zone. Due to the *pullback* and quietness of the stock, it can also go in the opposite direction in an attempt to increase volatility. This type of setup makes it hard to get into pre-breakout because we aren't 100% sure of the direction. Guessing the breakout direction can stop out traders of a winning setup.

Pro-Tips

The trick to playing this setup as best as possible, is to try and play the *pullback* after the move happens. The reason for this is because when a stock increases in volatility all of a sudden, it normally doesn't continue in the breakout direction forever. A healthy reaction will be for the stock to make a quick *pullback*, maybe a *gap fills*, or moving average touch. Another strategy for options traders is to buy a *strangle/straddle*, buying calls and puts, and hope time decay doesn't eat you alive before the move. For an option trader to make money in a *straddle*, they just need one direction to produce at least a 100% return. The move above was Amazon, and the call option ended up moving 300%. The resulting profit was only 200% because the put option is basically worthless. But in return for lower overall gains, you were prepared for a move in any direction.

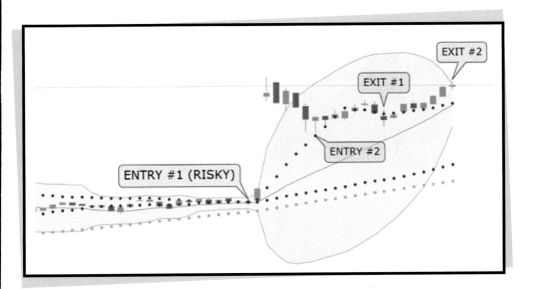

Where to Enter

The risky place to enter this setup is pre breakout, which could be when the *bollinger bands* get extremely close, when the price keeps sitting on the mid *bollinger band* (as the example above), when price touches the bottom *bollinger band*, or when price touches the slowest moving average. Again because we don't know the direction of the breakout, this can be very risky. The safer place to enter this setup is once price breaks out. But again, this can be tough if price *gaps* higher; playing *gaps* is never easy for traders. For this setup, the best *pullback* entry point could be a touch of the ten moving average (entry #2).

Where to Place Stop

The stop loss should be placed below the slowest moving average (yellow) for entry #1 and below the fastest moving average (purple) for entry #2. The amount that traders risk is fully dependent on how much they think they can make.

Where to Take Profit

The best place to take profit is when price touches the upper bollinger (exit #2) band or when price crosses the ten moving average (exit #1). In the example above, traders would have made more by exiting at exit #2.

Trend Pullback and Bounce off 200 Moving Average

27

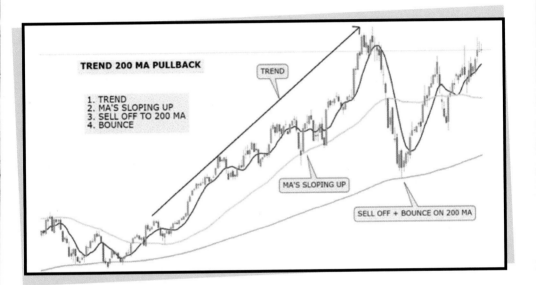

TREND 200 MA PULLBACK

1. TREND
2. MA'S SLOPING UP
3. SELL OFF TO 200 MA
4. BOUNCE

TREND

MA'S SLOPING UP

SELL OFF + BOUNCE ON 200 MA

Setup Explained

This setup requires a strong trend, which can be seen by all of the moving averages sloping up (10-purple, 50-yellow, 200-blue). Like most strong trends, the first real *pullback* will be large and will offer traders the ideal entry point to get into the trend. This entry point will be at the 200 moving average. This only works if the 200 moving average is sloping up at the time of the *pullback* and we see *confirmation* that buyers are coming in. Again, a *pullback* this large means more *consolidation* in the future and maybe a retest of the previous highs. A *pullback* of this magnitude shows the buyers are extremely weak and likely not able to continue the trend as easily as before.

Why it works

Just like bulletproof setup #8 with the *pullback* to the *bollinger band*, this is a similar situation, and an area buyers likely defend on any *pullback* after a strong trend. The reason this works, is that in general, the 200 moving average has 200 prices averaged in. A moving average represents the fair short or long term value of the stock, depending on the moving average length. The 200 moving average, in turn, is the fairest longest term value of the stock because of all that price averaged in, meaning it is a very attractive price for buyers or sellers to defend. Not to mention this is the most scanned moving average, the most traded, the most talked about on CNBC, and really the most popular. With all the attention already on it, there is no surprise that people are always buying or selling when price touches it.

Warnings

As you can see from the example above, the first small pullback only made it to the yellow moving average before popping (ma's sloping up). The problem with playing *pullbacks* is, it may never get to the perfect level (200 moving average), and you may need to improvise. Just an example, the SPY touched the 200-day moving average in 2016 and didn't pull back to it again until 2018. Another warning about this setup is that nobody likes to buy the *pullback* after a large trend. This is because it is littered with fear and doubt, trade wars, interest rate hikes, or impeachment. The best traders know the news and fear just helps the big players snatch up shares from *weak hands*. Change your mindset with these moments and avoid being the *weak hands*.

Pro-Tips

As stated earlier, recognize when fear is irrational and capitalize on it. There are few times in the market, a large trend pulls back to the 200 moving average, and when this happens, you don't have time to be emotional. As a trader, whenever I think news and fear will overrule a time tested setup, I am wrong. Great setups defy logic, emotions, and news for the most part.

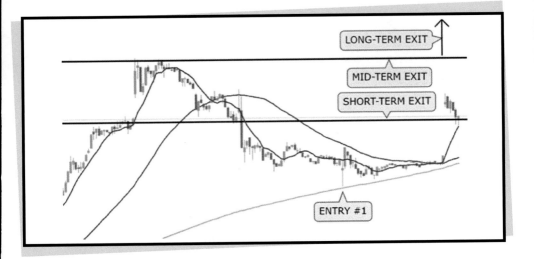

Where to Enter

The entry is very simple for this setup, as close to the 200 moving average as possible (entry #1). This will normally be a place of high *support* and lead to a continuation of the trend.

Where to Place Stop

The stop loss should be placed below the 200 moving average. The amount that traders risk is fully dependent on how much they think they can make.

Where to Take Profit

The best short-term exit is the first consolidation zone or 50% *retracement* of the prior move. The mid-term exit is going to be a 100% *retracement* of the preceding move. The long-term exit may be a break to new highs and a continuation of the trend.

Reversal and 10 Moving Average Curl

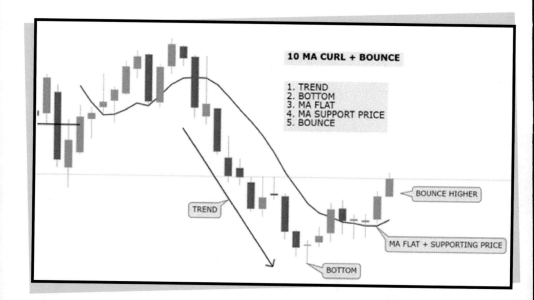

28

Setup Explained

For this setup to work well, we need a strong trend, a bottom of that trend, then a pop above the ten moving average. If the stock gets above the ten moving average and spends enough time above it, the moving average should eventually flatten out and *support* price. At this point, it is the ideal place to enter this trade. We have confirmation of the bottom, we have *support* from the moving average, and ideally, the stock will pop off this quickly.

Why it works

For a strong selling trend in the market, the ten moving average will be sloping down aggressively; the reaction to the bottom of this trend produces a quick move hopefully above the ten moving average. The ten moving average visually shows the trend of the stock in the exact moment. So for it to be sloping down during the whole sell-off, we know the direction is bearish. Once we bottom and see that moving average flatten out, now we have proof the direction is no longer down but flat. Any pop at this point has the possibility of now turning that moving average up and starting a new trend.

Warnings

When the price is sitting on the ten moving average, there will be attempts to drop lower, it is important to have some confidence in pattern and avoid getting *stopped out*. It takes time to shake out the sellers but after that happens, the buyers are free and clear. It can't be said enough that this moving average needs to flatten out, so the price can sit on top of it. Another mistake most traders make is playing the first candle that sits on the moving average, the key is to wait for multiple candles to find *support* there. This just further shows the strength of the buyers weakening the sellers.

Pro-Tips

This reversal play only works well if we have a strong trend. This is because strong trends lead to emotions and especially at the bottom of a trend this could mean a huge reversal very suddenly. That is why this play works so well. This quick reversal puts price above the ten moving average which allows traders to capitalize on the *support* and possible continuation higher. This pop off the ten moving average tends to hit resistance first at the mid *bollinger band*, so the larger the gap between them, the more the possible profit.

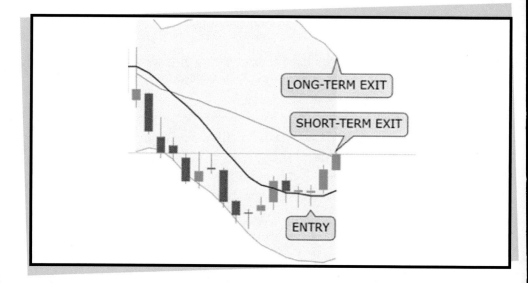

Where to Enter

The best place to enter the moving average curl is when the price starts sitting on the moving average (entry #1). This can be seen by the entry above and it is important to note that it is better to wait for the second or third candle to find support on the moving average.

Where to Place Stop

The stop loss should be placed below the ten moving average (purple line). The amount that traders risk is fully dependent on how much they think they can make.

Where to Take Profit

The best place to take profit is usually based on *bollinger band* levels. The two key levels for this are the mid *bollinger band* (short-term exit) and the upper *bollinger band* (long-term exit). Like previous examples, you could also use 50 or 100% *retracement* levels too.

Moving Average Twist

29

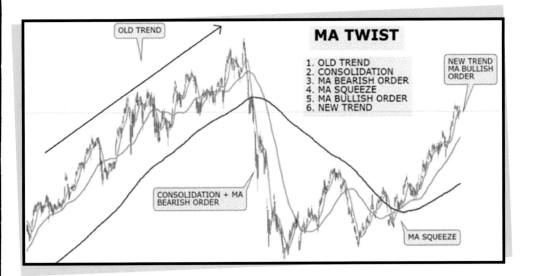

MA TWIST

1. OLD TREND
2. CONSOLIDATION
3. MA BEARISH ORDER
4. MA SQUEEZE
5. MA BULLISH ORDER
6. NEW TREND

OLD TREND

NEW TREND
MA BULLISH
ORDER

CONSOLIDATION + MA
BEARISH ORDER

MA SQUEEZE

Setup Explained

In a trend, we see moving averages start to slope up and spread apart. Eventually, the stock needs to consolidate to bring these moving averages back together. This is exactly what happens above, and eventually, they all twist together or just get really close. Once the moving averages converge (come together) or twist (cross each other), then the trend begins again in the initial direction. It is also important to note the moving average order during the bullish move, drop, *consolidation*, and new bullish trend. In both bullish trends, we see the moving averages stacked from fastest to slowest (orange, green, purple- top to bottom). In the bearish drop, we see the opposite, which is the slowest on top of the fastest (purple, orange, green- top to bottom). In *consolidation*, we start seeing all the moving averages consistently crossing each other; this is a sign of no direction. Lastly, the moving averages reorder themselves in a *bullish order*, just like the initial trend earlier.

Why it works

In trends, moving averages start spreading apart because some are slow and some are fast. This is unsustainable, as stated earlier, and each line represents fair value of the stock for a different length of time. Stocks need to pull back or consolidate to bring long term fair value closer to short term fair value. We can also think of moving averages like magnets, and the further price gets away from them, the harder it is to continue the trend. The reason this setup is a *consolidation* and continuation setup is that the moving averages stay flat the whole time during *consolidation*. This is the perfect moment. Once the moving averages come together, that is right when the breakout should begin because long term / short term fair value is finally aligned. Now buyers from everywhere start showing interest at these levels. Sometimes, you may get a twist/convergence in the moving averages. After this point, we start seeing some of the faster moving averages sloping up. This is the ultimate sign the stock is ready to rip, because theoretically there is no *resistance* above, as the price is above all moving averages now.

Warnings

Be very careful playing this before the moving averages are stacked in a bullish order. There could still be a lot of *chopping* ahead, which may lead to stop losses being hit. Also, be aware of the slopes of all the moving averages. The breakout becomes imminent when they start going completely flat or start pointing up. If these conditions are not met the stock may actually fall lower.

Pro-Tips

When you see the moving averages stacked in a bullish or bearish way, this is the easiest way to spot the trend. Just in this chart alone, a trader could have played the uptrend, downtrend, and new uptrend. Options traders could make a killing by using the *straddle* option strategy, only after the moving averages come together entirely or all flatten out. When you are never 100% sure of the breakout direction, most traders will buy calls and puts. This eliminates the guessing game, and because the probability of a large move is high, you only need one option leg to move more than 100% to make money.

Just in this setup alone, you could have made 300-500%. Even with the put option becoming worthless, you are still up 200-400%. Not a bad day.

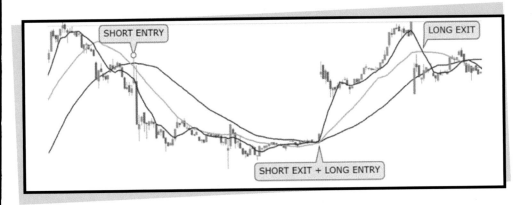

Where to Enter

The idea is that when the moving averages stack up in a *bearish order* (slow, medium, fast - top to bottom), that is when traders will enter *short* positions (*short* entry). The best place to enter *long* positions is when moving averages stack up in a *bullish order* (slow, medium, fast - bottom to top), as seen by the *long* entry above.

Where to Place Stop

The stop loss should be placed above the slowest moving average (pink) for the *short* setup and below the slowest moving average for the *long* setup. The amount that traders risk is fully dependent on how much they think they can make.

Where to Take Profit

The best place to exit these positions is when the moving averages cross. For example, the slow cross the medium, fast crosses slow, or basically when a whole new order begins (bearish to bullish). This can be seen above by the *short* exit and *long* exit.

Bulletproof Next Steps

Options Basic Course (Free)

Matt has spent most of his trading life mastering options. Options trading allows traders to leverage their small accounts to make some serious profit. Not only that, but long term investors use options to hedge during market uncertainty. As 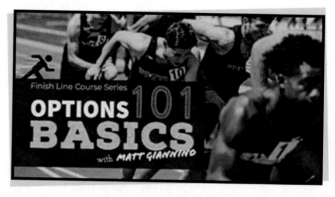 well as create a passive income by selling options against their positions. Those skills only come after learning the basics, and because Matt believes in the power of options so much, he decided to make this course completely free.

https://www.marketmovesmatt.com/options-basics

Premium Option Alerts (7 Day Free Trial)

Matt mentors, teaches, and gives his best trades to hundreds of options traders every single week. His track record tops most option alert services, and he strives to bring excellence to this group every second. But this group offers so much more. If you decide to take him up on the seven-day free trial, you will receive 3-5 option swing trades a week, 5-10 killer charts, text message alerts, private chat group, unlimited mentorship, two charting live streams, early bird discounted access to all new products, and so much more. Most traders who join never want to leave and on average stay for 4-6 months. If you want your seven days for free click the link below.

https://www.marketmovesmatt.com/trade-alert-special

Market Domination Course

Matt constantly gets phone calls where traders ask to be mentored by him. Although he constantly teaches in his premium group, he has stopped taking one-on-one clients because of a lack of time. This is incredibly tough because Matt wants to get traders to the next level. This is where Market Domination came about, and this is a 100+ video course where you can get every ounce of knowledge from Matt's mind for a fraction of the cost of mentoring sessions.

These 100+ videos take traders through:

- Indicators
- Time frames
- Moving averages
- Charting
- Candlesticks
- Options
- Entering Buy/Sell Orders
- Option spreads
- Fundamental analysis
- Technical analysis
- 10 Expert Trading Strategies
- Long Term Investing Tactics

Market domination is the most thorough trading course on the internet, and the best part is, it comes with **6 months in his options trading group ($936 value for free).**

https://www.marketmovesmatt.com/market-domination

Disclaimer

NONE OF GIANNINO PRODUCTS AND SERVICES LLC, ITS OWNERS (EXPRESSLY INCLUDING BUT NOT LIMITED), OFFICERS, DIRECTORS, EMPLOYEES, SUBSIDIARIES, AFFILIATES, LICENSORS, SERVICE PROVIDERS, CONTENT PROVIDERS AND AGENTS (ALL COLLECTIVELY HEREINAFTER REFERRED TO AS Giannino Products and Services LLC) AND ARE NOT FINANCIAL ADVISERS AND NOTHING CONTAINED HEREIN IS INTENDED TO BE OR TO BE CONSTRUED AS FINANCIAL ADVICE. "Giannino Products and Services LLC IS NOT AN INVESTMENT ADVISORY SERVICE, IT EXIST FOR EDUCATIONAL PURPOSES ONLY, AND THE MATERIALS AND INFORMATION CONTAINED HEREIN ARE FOR GENERAL INFORMATIONAL PURPOSES ONLY. NONE OF THE INFORMATION PROVIDED IN THE WEBSITE IS INTENDED AS INVESTMENT, TAX, ACCOUNTING OR LEGAL ADVICE, AS AN OFFER OR SOLICITATION OF AN OFFER TO BUY OR SELL, OR AS AN ENDORSEMENT, RECOMMENDATION OR SPONSORSHIP OF ANY COMPANY, PRODUCT OR SERVICE. THE INFORMATION ON THE WEBSITE SHOULD NOT BE RELIED UPON FOR PURPOSES OF TRANSACTING, TRADING OR INVESTING. YOU HEREBY UNDERSTAND AND AGREE THAT Giannino Products and Services LLC, DOES NOT OFFER OR PROVIDE TAX, LEGAL OR INVESTMENT ADVICE AND THAT YOU ARE RESPONSIBLE FOR CONSULTING TAX, LEGAL, DEALERS OR FINANCIAL PROFESSIONALS BEFORE ACTING ON ANY INFORMATION PROVIDED HEREIN."THIS REPORT IS NOT INTENDED AS A PROMOTION OF ANY PARTICULAR PRODUCTS OR INVESTMENTS, AND NEITHER LT NOR ANY OF ITS OFFICERS, DIRECTORS, EMPLOYEES OR REPRESENTATIVES,IN ANY WAY RECOMMENDS OR ENDORSES ANY COMPANY, PRODUCT, INVESTMENT OR OPPORTUNITY WHICH MAY BE DISCUSSED HEREIN. THE EDUCATION AND

Giannino Products and Services LLC does not receive any compensation from any party concerning any stocks or securities mentioned or traded in any of its services.

All content displayed is entirely informational, and is not suggested or intended to replace skilled research, advice or guidance from licensed investors or otherwise.

All information provided is for education purposes only. Giannino Products and Services LLC is not an advisory service or a registered investment broker-dealer. We may hold positions in stocks, options, and other market instruments discussed, but this in no way constitutes investment advice.

All trades and positions posted and/or discussed by the chat room moderator are neither a solicitation to buy or sell a particular security or market instrument, nor are they investment advice.

Giannino Products and Services LLC live trading room, chart examples, webinars, videos, mentoring, emails and any other content on this website is for the sole purpose of education and information, and should not be construed as investment advice. We do not provide tax or legal advice as it relates to stock trading, please refer to a qualified professional for these services.

Trading the markets in any capacity involves substantial risk of loss. This activity may not be appropriate for everyone, and you should only risk what you can afford to lose. Giannino Products and Services LLC does not guarantee trading profits, nor do we guarantee freedom from risk. You must assess the risk of any trade with your broker or financial professional and then make your own independent decisions regarding any trades taken. Giannino Products and Services LLC is in no way responsible or liable for any trader losses whatsoever.